THE RIGHT WAY TO
WRITE YOUR OWN CV

In the same series – Uniform with this book

'The Job's Yours!' – Handbook of a Proven Successful Job
    Search Strategy
General & Social Letter Writing
Positive Selling
The Polite Approach – A Handbook of Etiquette

In the Right Way Series – Larger format paperbacks

When Do I Start? – The Definitive Guide to Job-Hunting
    Success

THE RIGHT WAY TO
WRITE YOUR OWN CV

by

John Clarke MIMgt

PAPERFRONTS

Typeset in 10/11pt Times by County Typesetters, Margate, Kent.
Printed and bound in Great Britain by Cox & Wyman Ltd., Reading, Berkshire.

The *Paperfronts* series and the *Right Way* series are both published by Elliot Right Way Books, Brighton Road, Lower Kingswood, Tadworth, Surrey, KT20 6TD, U.K.

CONTENTS

For Jenifer

INTRODUCTION

The challenges of the twenty-first century are going to prove more exciting for some than for others. Technological progress will continue to offer great opportunities and an improved life style to those in the forefront. Others will find a steadily declining demand for their services, as computer brains encroach further into the workplace. Permanently high levels of unemployment throughout the civilised world are turning job applicants into competitors for a prize: the prize being the job at the end of it all. This is where the CV comes into focus.

While many people have a vague idea of how to put a CV together, those who have gone thoroughly into the whys and wherefores beforehand are much more likely to be invited to an interview. A rather unfortunate pitfall awaiting applicants who are making a genuine, all-out effort is the poor quality of advice bandied about by so-called 'experts'. This can lead applicants to undersell themselves disastrously, by causing them to offer too little information.

The purpose of this book is to provide an easy-to-follow guide. I do not claim that it will overcome all the problems. No book could. Each one of us is unique, and nowhere is that fact more clearly displayed than in a bundle of CVs where the career patterns of people who have worked in the same trade or profession can be infinitely variable.

Views vary about the layout of a CV, but the method shown in the pages of this book has achieved outstanding results, time and time again.

First, read the book carefully right through. Then,

return to the beginning and start composing the CV. Read a bit and do a bit, then read a bit more and so on, to the end.

I have addressed the book to the male readers, in order to avoid the awful he/she option at every point, but all that is said in the book is equally applicable to my lady readers.

I start by showing an unrealistically simple, completed specimen CV. This deliberate over-simplification brings the essential points to the fore.

PERSONAL DETAILS

Full Name:	Sarah Jones
Address:	101 Heron Road, Anytown, Midshire, XX1 1YY
Telephone No:	Anytown (01888) 888888
Date of Birth:	9th August (year)
Place of Birth:	Anytown, Midshire
Nationality:	British
Marital Status:	Single – no children
Driving Licence:	Current (clean)

CURRICULUM VITAE

EDUCATION AND QUALIFICATIONS

Sept. (year) Anytown Comprehensive School
– July (year) Anytown, Midshire

June (year) GCSE

Mathematics	(A)
English	(B)
(Oral Communication	2)
Business Studies	(B)
Information Technology	(B)
Geography	(C)
History	(C)

Sept. (year) Anytown College of Further and Higher
– June (year) Education, Anytown, Midshire
– Evening Classes

Royal Society of Arts
June (year) RSA 1 – Word Processing

National Vocational Qualification
June (year)
NVQ Level 3 – Business Administration

TRAINING

Acme Retail Ltd
Oct. (year) Induction (1 week)
Nov. (year) Stock Ordering (1 day)
Jan. (year) Office Procedures (3 days)

EXPERIENCE

Oct. (year) Acme Retail Ltd
– to date 66–68 High Street, Anytown, Midshire
– Retailers of Ladies' Fashions

Administration Clerk – daily updating of
sales charts; completing stock discrepancy
forms; balancing tills; banking; ordering
stationery; processing correspondence.

Apr. (year) Porter & Clegg Ltd
– Oct. (year) Beacon Road, Crossley Industrial Estate,
Anytown, Midshire
– Wholesalers of Paint and Wall Coverings

Assistant Stock Control Clerk – checking
incoming stock; verifying invoices;

typing customer invoices; assisting with
preparations for audits.

July (year)	Anytown Estates
– Apr. (year)	90 Leamington Road, Anytown, Midshire
	– Estate Agents and Valuers
	Trainee Clerk.

OUTSIDE ACTIVITIES

Hobbies   Walking, aerobics and dancing.

References   Available on request.

1
PERSONAL DETAILS

We will begin by dealing with this section of the CV, not only because it comes first, but also because with all CVs the arrangement of the personal details will be similar. Any differences are confined to the amount of information given.

For instance, where the applicant intends to apply for employment in a particular role, e.g. electrician, the personal details will contain the firm statement that that is what he is, and the fact will then be displayed thus:

Occupation: Electrician – JIB Approved.

The purpose behind this inclusion is to make the reader aware at an early stage that here is a specialist, and not a jack-of-all-trades prepared to try his hand at anything. But beware, because if it is anticipated that a broad range of vacancies might be applied for, the CV may not serve its purpose with the occupation inserted, and the applicant could find himself severely restricted. If this seems likely, no occupation should be included in the personal details.

If the CV is being prepared with a view to applying for a single job vacancy, and is not likely to be used again in the foreseeable future, the applicant's age will appear alongside date of birth. This will reduce the reading time, by eliminating the need for the reader to test his powers of mental arithmetic.

When the CV is likely to be used over a long period, the actual age should not be inserted because the passage of time will eventually create an inaccuracy. Although, if you keep your CV on a word processor/computer you can, of course, update it each time you send it out. However, remember that companies and recruitment agencies frequently hold CVs on file for many months before making a response, so any ages given will go out-of-date.

Although of less importance, the entry giving details about the number and ages of children can also become out-of-date. For this reason, some applicants prefer to give the children's dates of birth only.

Next of kin is a detail which can be needed, particularly if dangerous work or employment overseas is the goal. This is most appropriate in the case of a single or divorced person.

Another sub-heading which might not be used in every instance covers state of health. This applies if physical fitness is likely to be a consideration of more than average importance, e.g. a physical training instructor at a holiday camp, or any post demanding prolonged physical exertion, particularly in climates where extremes of temperature prevail.

Ideally, this aspect of the personal details will be dealt with by declaring the possession of a current medical certificate. People whose leisure pursuits require them to have regular medical checks might also hold a certificate of fitness.

Medical Certificate: Valid to August (year).

Or if no medical certificate is available, the entry will read:

Health: Excellent.

(Assuming, of course, that the physical state accords with the entry.)

Showing that the driving licence is clean can say something about a person, and not just that he has had luck on his side. If the job being applied for involves using a company vehicle, a clean licence can be a positive advantage. If the licence is not free from points, the entry will read: Current (full) – assuming that a full licence has been obtained.

If the subject wishes it to be known that he is prepared to relocate, a sub-heading entitled Preferred Location will be included. This might say: Prepared to relocate within the UK. Alternatively, if the applicant wishes to leave open the question of relocation, but desires to enhance his prospects of an interview, he might say: Prepared to work anywhere in the UK, thus leaving himself free to state on some future occasion that he will travel home each weekend. However, it is by no means certain that a prospective employer would accept the latter as an alternative to relocation.

Many people seek work abroad for a variety of reasons. Preferred location might then read: Prepared to work anywhere in the world. Obviously, the question of returning home each weekend would not arise in this case. Those who wish to work abroad, but have no previous experience, would do well to remember the reaction of the gentleman who, having returned from a winter in the Falkland Islands, amended his preferred location to read: Prepared to work in any warm country.

Where the applicant does not wish to relocate, under any circumstances, preferring to work within commuting distance, the preferred location sub-heading should not be used.

Sometimes more details are needed. Try to remember the requirements of application forms relating to your own trade, profession or aspirations. For example, in certain foreign parts an applicant may be required to declare his religion. To minimise the risk of a clash of religious beliefs, most seasoned campaigners to foreign parts simply put Christian, and leave it at that.

The national insurance number is always an inclusion when the CV is being used to apply for work offshore. Again, it is a matter of knowing your own field.

Apart from the items already discussed, the personal

details should be presented as in the example below. To some readers, this list may appear to be inordinately large. The reason for its apparent bulk is the need for me to display all the sub-headings which are likely to appear in a CV. It goes almost without saying that few, if any, applicants will require them all. For instance, a person who does not possess a passport is not expected to insert the appropriate sub-heading only to leave a blank space alongside. Neither will he use the passport sub-heading, if he is not likely to be going abroad in his work.

PERSONAL DETAILS

Full Name:	James Smith
Occupation:	Electrician – JIB Approved
Address:	1 The Close, Anytown, Midshire, XX1 1YY
Telephone No:	Anytown (01888) 888888
Date of Birth:	15th February (year). (Age – XX.)
Place of Birth:	Anytown, Midshire
Nationality:	British
Religion:	Christian
Marital Status:	Married with son aged 11 and daughter aged 6.
Next of Kin:	Mrs A Smith (wife) – address as above.
Nat. Ins. No:	ZZ 00 00 00 Z
Driving Licence:	Current (full)
Passport No:	X 888888 Y – expires October (year)
Health:	Excellent
Preferred Location:	Prepared to work anywhere in the world.

2
EDUCATION, QUALIFICATIONS AND TRAINING

Like the career details, this section varies from one individual to the next. I have constructed these five examples in such a way as to cover the essentials that all applicants will need.

Education, from the age of eleven onward, should be included. It is common for an applicant to have attended more than one school during these years, therefore we might commence with:

EDUCATION AND QUALIFICATIONS

Sept. (year)   Anytown Comprehensive School
– July (year)   Anytown, Midshire

Sept. (year)   Hightown High School
– July (year)   Hightown, Midshire

Where an applicant has attended more than two schools (I once had a client who had been to nine), it is standard practice to include only the last two.

After showing the school or schools attended, we come to the examination successes and might then proceed as follows:

June (year)   GCSE
Mathematics	(C)
English	(C)
(Oral Communication	2)
Home Economics	(C)
Computer Studies	(D)
Physics	(D)
Biology	(E)

Those born before 1972, should give their GCE 'O' Level and/or CSE subjects with grades.

It is generally preferable to present these lists in descending order of grades or pass, although where a particular subject, or subjects, is of greater importance in relation to the kind of work being sought it may be prudent to depart from this practice.

An applicant who has received no further formal training would proceed to the presentation of his career history. However, for the benefit of those who have gone on to further education, we will continue.

Sept. (year)   Anytown College of Further and Higher
– June (year) Education, Anytown, Midshire
                     – Full-time

(Unlike this course, others might require only part-time attendance, e.g. Day Release, Block Release or Evening Classes – state which.)

June (year)   BTEC National Diploma
– Hotel, Catering and Institutional Operations
(17 Units: 3 Distinctions; 12 Merits; 2 Passes)

June (year)   BTEC HND
– Hotel, Catering and Institutional Management
(18 Units: 10 Merits; 8 Passes)

Where a long list of certificates and diplomas has been obtained, the question sometimes arises: need all of them be listed, or does the final one or possibly the last two outweigh the earlier ones to the point of making them superfluous? This is a question which the applicant will often be able to answer himself. If not, specialist advice should be sought and where doubt still remains, all certificates should be listed. In the case of the HND which we are dealing with here, it is necessary to decide whether it would be worthwhile providing a breakdown of the programme, listing the units passed with the grade of pass obtained in each unit. Whatever the particular field of endeavour may be, this question will always arise with regard to the most advanced qualification gained, because in most cases the recipient of the CV will have little or no knowledge of the course content.

All right, so what do we do? In this instance, I would first find out if the applicant possessed the level of experience to match his HND. If he did, I would prefer to leave things as they stand and use the space saved on the CV to expand on his career history. If he did not possess an adequate range and depth of experience, I would list the units passed, taking them together with the levels and grades of pass straight off the diploma, or its accompanying notification of performance. The need to do this is most common where applicants are of a young age, and have not had the time to develop their careers to any great extent. When facing this dilemma, many applicants place photocopies of their certificates and associated documentation in the envelope with their CV. The resulting bulge of unsolicited material is likely to discourage the recruiter, whose desk may already be piled high with the efforts of others. Far better to have an extra page on the CV, which might at least command respect on account of the time and patience that has obviously been required.

Industrial placements or college placements, whatever their duration, should be treated as a normal job in the career history, with the fact clearly stated in each case, e.g.:

June (year)　The George Hotel
– Sept. (year)　125 South Promenade, Anytown, Midshire
　　　　　　　　– Fully licensed residential hotel
　　　　　　　　(45 bedrooms – en suite).

　　　　　　　　Management Trainee on industrial placement.
　　　　　　　　Receptionist – receiving guests; handling telephone enquiries; operating a computerised reservations and accounts system.

　If the HND was obtained some years ago, it may not be necessary to include the industrial placements, on account of the experience now gained.

　　　　　　　Royal Institute of Public Health and Hygiene
　　　　　　　June (year)
　　　　　　　The Food Hygiene and Handling Certificate

　Even if this was obtained before the HND, it will come as the last entry in education and qualifications, in order to avoid interrupting the flow of OND and HND information.

　Over the years, many applicants will have attended short training courses, run either by the employing company or a specialist training organisation. Where these are at all likely to have a bearing on future employment, they should be included at this point on the CV.

TRAINING

　　　　　　　Global Hotels plc
June (year)　Organising Functions　(1 week)
Jan. (year)　Interviewing　　　　(3 days)
Feb. (year)　Problem Analysis　　(1 week)

It is worth mentioning here, that recruitment agencies tend to rely on key words and phrases when retrieving potential candidates from their databases, e.g. AUTO-CAD, TQM, BS 5750, just-in-time, etc. Sometimes relevant courses (involving these key words) will have been attended, so it is important to include them. Where the involvement has been by way of practical experience, the inclusion will go into the career history section.

This tendency to use key words seems to be most common in the very broad field of engineering, but whatever the occupation, it is a good idea to try and keep pace with the latest techniques and terminology, especially if the CV is going to agencies.

Where an applicant is a member of a professional association, the appropriate entry should be made here, e.g.:

Professional Association
     MHCIMA

Where this entry is applicable, it is worth considering whether to include the letters of the professional association alongside your full name in personal details. Although some applicants think it might appear boastful, doing this does convey an instant message to the reader. The same consideration should be given in the case of a degree, e.g. BA (Hons).

This applicant's education, qualifications and training section is now complete, as follows:

EDUCATION AND QUALIFICATIONS

Sept. (year)   Anytown Comprehensive School
– July (year)   Anytown, Midshire

Sept. (year)   Hightown High School
– July (year)   Hightown, Midshire

June (year)   GCSE
Mathematics   (C)
English   (C)
(Oral Communication   2)
Home Economics   (C)
Computer Studies   (D)
Physics   (D)
Biology   (E)

Sept. (year)   Anytown College of Further and Higher
– June (year) Education, Anytown, Midshire
                 – Full-time

June (year)   BTEC National Diploma
– Hotel, Catering and Institutional
Operations
(17 Units: 3 Distinctions; 12 Merits; 2 Passes)

June (year)   BTEC HND
– Hotel, Catering and Institutional
Management
(18 Units: 10 Merits; 8 Passes)

Royal Institute of Public Health and Hygiene
June (year)
The Food Hygiene and Handling
Certificate

TRAINING

Global Hotels plc
June (year)   Organising Functions   (1 week)
Jan. (year)   Interviewing   (3 days)
Feb. (year)   Problem Analysis   (1 week)

Professional Association
            MHCIMA

Next comes the less typical case of the applicant whose further education and training is a mix between civilian and military. Anyone who has served in HM Armed Forces should find this example helpful:

EDUCATION AND QUALIFICATIONS

Sept. (year)   Anytown School
– July (year)   Anytown, Midshire

               June (year)   CSE
               Technical Drawing   (2)
               Mathematics   (2)
               English   (4)

Sept. (year)   Anytown College of Technology
– June (year)   Anytown, Midshire
               – Day Release

               City and Guilds of London Institute
               – Heavy and Light Vehicle Maintenance
               June (year)   Part One Certificate
               June (year)   Part Two Certificate

(Year) – (year)   Royal Air Force (Service Qualifications)
               (Year)
               Education Test Certificate – Part Two
               – English; Geography; History.

TRAINING

(Year)   Instructional Techniques.
               Forward Reporting.
               Recruiting.
               Emergency Services Vehicle Maintenance.
               Basic Computing.

Setting out the education and qualifications in the way I have shown, i.e. displaying the qualifications immediately below the school, college, university or other establishment at which they were gained, is unfortunately not always practicable. When an applicant has attended numerous colleges and gained separate qualifications at each one, the list becomes so spread out that it has to be handled differently, albeit less satisfactorily:

EDUCATION

Sept. (year)	Anytown Comprehensive School
– July (year)	Anytown, Midshire
Sept. (year)	Anytown College of Further and Higher
– June (year)	Education, Anytown, Midshire
	– Full-time
Sept. (year)	Hightown College of Further and Higher
– June (year)	Education, Hightown, Midshire
	– Day Release and Evening Classes
Oct. (year)	Anytown University
– June (year)	Anytown, Midshire
	– Full-time

QUALIFICATIONS

June (year)	*GCE 'O' Level*
Mathematics	(A)
English Language	(B)
Physics	(B)
History	(B)
Art and Design	(B)

Geography   (C)
French   (D)

June (year)   ONC – Electronics
(18 Units: 8 Merits; 5 Passes; 5 Exempt)

June (year)   HNC – Electronics
(10 Units: 2 Distinctions; 6 Merits; 2 Passes)

June (year)   B Eng (Hons) – II (ii)

Obviously, the aim here is to economise on space, while still providing the necessary information. However, the question still arises of whether or not to give a course breakdown of the most advanced qualification, in this instance, a degree. In making this decision, you have to bear in mind that the syllabus of one institution may vary from that of another, in the same subject. Unless the recipient of the CV has copies of the different syllabuses readily to hand, confusion could arise. Advice on this should be available to those attending university.

The example shown below assumes that the applicant has graduated from university with a degree in law and is applying for articles, prior to attending law school. This applicant provides a year by year breakdown of the degree course.

EDUCATION AND QUALIFICATIONS

Sept. (year)   Anytown School
– July (year)   Anytown, Midshire

June (year)   GCSE
English   (A)
(Oral Communication   1)

Mathematics	(A)
English Literature	(B)
Geography	(B)
History	(B)
Biology	(B)
Chemistry	(C)

June (year)	*GCE 'A' Level*
Economics	*(A)*
English	*(A)*
General Studies	*(B)*
Geography	*(C)*

Oct. (year)   University of Anyborough
– June (year)

June (year)   *LLB (Hons) – II (ii)*

1st Year
English Legal System; Tort; Contract Law;
Criminal Law; Constitutional Law.

2nd Year
Land Law; Equity and Trusts; Industrial
Law; Administrative Law.

3rd Year
Jurisprudence; Remedies; Family Law;
Civil Liberties.

Sept (year)   To attend Midshire College of Law.
– July (year)   (Final Examination)

Occasionally, the education, qualifications and training might be set out in yet another way, because of the differing make up of the information, e.g.:

EDUCATION

Sept. (year)	Anytown Comprehensive School
– July (year)	Anytown, Midshire

QUALIFICATIONS

Nov. (year)	CITB Advanced Scaffolder's Card – Reg No: XXXXXX
Feb. (year)	NJC/ECI Registered Scaffolder No: XXXXXX
Aug. (year)	Permit User's Certificate No: XXXXXX
June (year)	TJIT Offshore Survival Certificate No: XXXXXX

TRAINING

	Cann Scaffolding (Anytown) Ltd	
Sept. (year)	Height Awareness	(3 days)
Feb. (year)	Health and Safety	(1 day)

The reason for the above layout is that there are no purely academic qualifications. This applicant's qualifications are a confirmation of the standards he is able to work to, and of his ability to survive an involuntary dip in the sea.

The preceding five examples of the different ways of approaching the task of setting out the education, qualifications and training section of a CV should provide a suitable structure for the majority of readers.

3
THE CAREER HISTORY
PART ONE

The career history is usually the part of a CV which most interests the reader. It is also the greatest in its demands of time, thought and patience on the part of the applicant.

You need to highlight the main duties and responsibilities of each job, and emphasise any notable achievements.

It is important to stick to the hard facts and to avoid small-talk, or statements which are merely conversational. Remember that the CV initially will get no more than a quick scan, perhaps lasting less than twenty seconds. Upon the impression given by that first acquaintance with the recruiter rests the decision as to whether the CV is placed on the small pile for a longer read later, or simply consigned to the waste-bin. Elegant flowing prose will impress no-one. The experienced recruiter will see straight through it and toss it aside with contempt.

There follow seven career history examples, each one followed by a question and answer table. Reading all of the examples should prove helpful to any applicant. It is important to understand the general style before applying the principles to your own history.

Do not use the first person (I/we). This greatly reduces the risk of appearing immodest, and enables you to make a strong, factual and concise presentation.

A LICENSEE

EXPERIENCE/ACHIEVEMENTS

Feb. (year) *– to date*	The Plough Hotel (Anyone's Brewery) Foxglove Road, Anytown, Midshire – 28 bedrooms (en suite) – 2 licensed bars – À la carte restaurant (80 covers) – Functions room

Licensed Manager responsible to the Area Manager for the day-to-day running of the business, including the recruitment, training and control of staff (32); organising weddings, parties, business conferences and Rotary functions for up to 120.

ACHIEVEMENT: Through improving public relations, making staff changes and applying tighter controls in all areas, a 15% increase in profitability was recorded in the first full year. This has been maintained.

June (year) *– Feb. (year)*	The Ship Tavern (Everyone's Brewery) Beach Road, Anytown, Midshire – 3 licensed bars – Dining-room with fast-food and full meals service (60 covers)

Licensed Manager responsible to the District Sales Manager for running the operation, including book-keeping, control of stock and cash and recruitment and training of staff (28). Catered for weddings, funerals, birthday parties and charity functions for up to 100.

Mar. (year) *– June (year)*	The White Lady Bars and Leisure Complex (Town House Leisure Co Ltd) The Promenade, Anytown, Midshire

Bars Manager responsible for running this busy, sea-front, multi-bar operation.
Public Bar: Up to 300 customers, demanding a rapid flow of alcoholic and soft drinks, as well as bar snacks.
Lounge Bar: Customers comprised a mixed concentration of locals and holidaymakers.
Cocktail Bar: Heavy lunch-time and late evening trade, from professional and business people.

Responsible for stock control and acquisition. Thirty-four full and part-time bar staff and cleaners.

Apr. (year) *– Mar. (year)*	The Manor Grill-Room Restaurant Olde Road, Anytown, Midshire – 75 covers – 1 licensed bar

Assistant Manager responsible for helping the Manager to achieve his objectives, and deputising in his absence.
Twenty-two full and part-time staff.

Aug. (year) *– Apr. (year)*	The Dog and Duck Inn (Middle West Brewery), Orchard Lane, Anytown, Midshire – Public House (3 bars)

Bartender – serving beers, shorts and cocktails to customers from all levels of society.

May (year) *– Aug. (year)*	Unemployed.

Nov. (year)   The Black Owl (Mountain Brewery)
– May (year) Anytown, Midshire
            – Fully licensed residential hotel
            – 55 bedrooms (en suite)

            Commis Chef – veg, larder and sweet.

Nov. (year)   The Olde Hall Inn (Free House)
– Nov. (year) Hall Lane, Anytown, Midshire

            Trainee Cellarman.

July (year)   Anytown Box Co Ltd
– Nov. (year) Shore Road, Anytown, Midshire

            Trainee Box Maker.

OUTSIDE ACTIVITIES

Hobbies   Football, squash and reading.

References Available on request.

Question: *Why does the career history read backwards?*

Answer: Because the present post will be of most interest to the reader, who will want to be able to form an accurate picture of the past ten years.

Question: *In his two most recent jobs, the applicant gives the job title of the person to whom he is responsible. In the other jobs he does not. Why?*

Answer: Because in those two jobs he is the manager of the entire site operation, and the reader will want to know how far up the ladder his line of communication reaches.

           In the other jobs it is obvious that he is either responsible to the manager (as in the positions of assistant manager and bars manager), or someone on the premises at assistant manager or supervisor level (as in the position of bartender). As a commis chef, he will be responsible to someone in the kitchen, probably the head chef or duty chef.

Whatever your role in your work might be, if you feel that additional emphasis can be given to the weight of responsibility that you carry, by including your immediate superior's job title, then go ahead. But remember, it will use up space and reading time.

Question: *This example covers more than ten years' employment. Why bother to go back so far?*

Answer: To show continuity of employment with no unexplained time gaps. Avoid allowing the reader to draw the conclusion that you might have been in prison or had serious health or mental problems for a time. If a period of unemployment took place a few years ago, show it. This is particularly important, where the last ten years are concerned.

Question: *What if the applicant is unable to recall the exact starting and finishing dates of his jobs?*

Answer: Do your best to put it all together, complete with month and year, for the past ten years. Beyond that, most applicants will only be able to recall the exact year, especially where many job changes have occurred.

In some cases, it may not be possible to set down all the jobs and employers in the accepted form. But you can still do a resumé as in the next example. (This question is given further coverage at the start of Chapter 7, Problems, Problems.)

A WORKSHOP MANAGER/
DIESEL ENGINE SPECIALIST

EXPERIENCE

Aug. (year) *– to date*	Bell & Bamber Transport Ltd Anytown Industrial Estate, Anytown, Midshire – 48 tractor units; 66 trailers Workshop Manager – running the workshop with seven skilled fitters and two office staff. Responsible for staff recruitment; adherence to strict maintenance schedules; 24–hour breakdown rota; acquisition of spares; checking invoices; ensuring compliance with health and safety regulations. Centrally involved in obtaining BS 5750 accreditation for the company.
Jan. (year) *– Aug. (year)*	Wheelways Marine Ltd 124–130 Dock Road, Anytown, Midshire – Road Haulage, Shipping and Warehousing – 150 articulated and rigid vehicles Fitter – repair and maintenance of diesel engines, transmissions, bodywork and trailers.
Oct. (year) *– Jan. (year)*	Unemployed.
Mar. (year) *– Oct. (year)*	Rance Leigh Construction (International) Plc, (Engineering and Plant Division), Hounds Road, Anytown, Midshire – Bangassou, Central Africa Workshop Foreman in charge of twenty-

eight mechanics, engaged in the repair and maintenance of all heavy and light vehicles on a dam and irrigation project. Ordered all spares; dealt with all workshop documentation.

Sept. (year)
– Mar. (year)   Western Road Services Ltd
Town Road, Anytown, Midshire
– Road Haulage Contractors (22 rigid vehicles)

Foreman Fitter – routine maintenance of commercial vehicles.

Jan. (year)
– Sept. (year)   Smith, Jones & Co Ltd
Bridgend Garage, Ford Lane, Anytown, Midshire
– Commercial Vehicle Distributors

Fitter – servicing new trucks.

(Year)
– (year)   Hillside Haulage and Repairs Ltd
Down Road, Anytown, Midshire

Diesel Mechanic – all types of commercial vehicle repairs.

(Year)
– (year)   UK & Foreign Technical Contracts
Employers Ltd, Capetown, South Africa
– South Africa and the Congo Basin

Diesel Mechanic – maintaining heavy vehicles engaged on dams, bridges, road works and forest clearance.

(Year)
– (year)   Diesel Mechanic with numerous companies including:

ABC Haulage Ltd
Rock Street, Anytown, Midshire

Move & Dump Ltd
Ashdown Street, Anytown, Midshire

Joe's Waste Disposal
Smith's Yard, Anytown, Midshire

Fire Engine Breakers and Renovations Ltd
Anytown, Midshire

West Midshire County Council
(Highways and Technical Services)

(Year)
– (year)

Anytown Construction Services Ltd (Plant
Division), Arkwright Road, Anytown,
Midshire

Apprentice Mechanic (Indentured) learning
all aspects of diesel powered vehicle and
plant repair and maintenance.

OUTSIDE ACTIVITIES

Hobbies   Cricket and vintage car restoration.

References   Available on request.

Question: *Will it not be damaging to the applicant's
                chances to have had so many jobs?*

Answer: To have had few jobs over a long period of
                time obviously shows a degree of stability
                and reliability, although skilled tradesmen
                who have had numerous employers have
                usually worked in places far apart and are
                accustomed to changes in working
                environment. This, coupled with the broad
                experience gained, will in many instances
                enhance their prospects.
                  Applicants should seek out jobs which
                match their CV.

Question: *Nowhere does this applicant give his reason for leaving. Why is this?*

Answer: While most job application forms request the answer to this question, it is unlikely the truth will always be told, especially in the case of the applicant who might have given his employer a black eye!

It is more effective to leave the reader with the impression that each job was superior to the previous one. Unfortunately, this is not always the case.

In the final analysis it is a matter for the individual to decide, but in stating the reason for leaving one job, he could feel obliged to do so for them all.

It is also as well to remember that whatever goes into a CV must be the truth, since it is a criminal offence to obtain employment by deception.

Question: *Why does the career history of this second example come under the heading Experience when in the previous one it came under Experience/Achievements?*

Answer: In the previous example, a particular achievement was singled out for special mention.

Question: *Why is the nature of the employer's business not fully stated every time?*

Answer: Where the nature of a company's business activities is adequately conveyed in the company name, to elaborate further would be a waste of space and reading time.

AN ELECTRICIAN – SEEKING WORK OFFSHORE

EXPERIENCE

June (year)
– to date

Anytown Management Services Ltd
– Contracting to Cann Oil

Approved Electrician on Cann 'B' Platform
– installation of electrical fire and gas
systems.

May (year)
– June (year)

Broadvale Engineering, Anytown

Approved Electrician on Morecambe Bay
hook-up – installation and commissioning of
fire and gas instrumentation; running and
terminating cables; wiring PA systems;
ladder racking and tray work.

Feb. (year)
– May (year)

RCN Electrical Contractors (Anytown) Ltd
– Midchester Leisure Centre

Approved Electrician – installation of heavy
gauge cable trunking.

Nov. (year)
– Feb. (year)

AMA Nuclear Systems Plc
– Norsham Power Station

Approved Electrician – installation and
testing of thermo-couples, strain gauges and
microphones.

Mar. (year)
– Nov. (year)

Hall & Rowe Ltd, Anytown
– New hypermarket for C&J

Approved Electrician – installation of
EPOS computer systems, emergency
lighting, via contactor controls; automatic
doors; zone fire alarm systems; steel wire
armoured cable.

Sept. (year)   BDR Construction (UK) Ltd
– Mar. (year) – Saudi Arabian Hospital Building Contract

Approved Electrician – installation of floor trunking and sockets; all theatre electrification; fire alarms; smoke and gas detection equipment.

June (year)   T & G Electrics (Anytown) Ltd
– Sept. (year) *June (year) – September (year)*
Electrician/Approved Electrician.

June (year) – June (year)
Apprentice Electrician (Indentured).

OUTSIDE ACTIVITIES

Hobbies   Keep Fit, Home Computing and DIY.

References   Available on request.

Question: *Why does this applicant not give the full addresses of his employers? Sometimes, he only gives the company's name.*

Answer: He is applying for work in the offshore oil and gas industry where recruitment staff will know most, if not all, of the companies shown in the CV. Furthermore, this industry is one of the most demanding in its need for a brief, but informative document.

Some of my clients even prefer not to use valuable space on items such as outside activities, or the mention of references. But that is their decision.

Where the applicant has limited offshore experience or none at all, he should give the addresses and main business activities of his employers in the usual way. His outside activities and his ability to provide references should also be shown briefly, as in the above example. The length of a CV is given further coverage on page 114 in Chapter 7, Problems, Problems.

Question: *Why bother to say that the apprenticeship was indentured?*

Answer: The quality of training given to apprentices varies and the possession of indentures (increasingly rare) will give a prospective employer more confidence, especially so in the case of a young applicant.

A MOTOR MECHANIC

– newly discharged from HM Armed forces and seeking work in civilian life.

EXPERIENCE

Oct. (year)   Army – Royal Electrical and Mechanical
– May (year)   Engineers.

> *July (year) – May (year)*
> Section Commander (UK) responsible for acquisition, control and inspection of all high and low cost items used in the repair and maintenance of tracked military vehicles.
> Twenty subordinate fitters and technicians.
>
> *April (year) – July (year)*
> Section Commander (Germany) – inspection and testing of wheeled military vehicles and the control and inspection of workshop equipment.
>
> *June (year) – April (year)*
> Corporal Mechanic (UN Forces – Cyprus) – control and acquisition of vehicle and equipment spare parts. Up to five subordinates.
>
> *October (year) – June (year)*
> Mechanic working in UK and Germany, carrying out major repairs to heavy plant. Much of this work was done in field conditions, where inaccessibility demanded frequent improvisation.
>
> *October (year) – October (year)*
> REME School – as above. [This will have been included in Education, Qualifications and Training.]

Certificate of Service reads: Conduct
Exemplary.
Rank on Discharge: Corporal.

Sept. (year)   Bardale Auto Services Ltd
– Oct. (year)   19–21 Avon Road, Anytown, Midshire

Apprentice Motor Mechanic – full-time in
the workshop while awaiting REME
service.

Summary   Extensive experience gained on a wide
range of light and heavy vehicles: petrol,
diesel, tracked and 4 × 4. Arc, MIG and
oxyacetylene welding.
Fitting and turning.
Refrigeration.
Air conditioning.
DC generators.

Objective   To become a Commercial Vehicle
Workshop Manager.

OUTSIDE ACTIVITIES

Hobbies   Snooker and fell walking.

References   Available on request.

Question: *This example shows that the applicant's most*
recent job has terminated, therefore he must
be unemployed. Is that not going to
jeopardise his chances?

Answer: Unfortunately yes, and the longer he
remains unemployed the worse his plight
will become. He must proceed immediately
to go flat out to find a job. Even if the new
job does not ideally match what he is
looking for, it will get him back on the
ladder and provide a firmer platform, from

which to apply for something more suitable.

Question: *Is it always a good idea to provide a summary of experience in this way?*

Answer: Only if you feel that the descriptions of your jobs cannot be made to convey enough of this kind of information without becoming too bulky. This question occurs most often with ex-Armed Forces and Merchant Navy personnel.

Question: *The Objective has not been included in previous examples. Why not?*

Answer: Because, as with Occupation in the personal details, a declared Objective could be binding if the applicant is likely to apply for a wide range of jobs.

Service in the Armed Forces will sometimes have been so involved that attempting to break it down into a conventional presentation would be impracticable. In such cases, a short narrative can be the best approach. E.g:

EXPERIENCE

Oct. (year)   Army – Royal Electrical and Mechanical
– May (year)   Engineers.

After twelve months at the REME School of Mechanical Engineering, a variety of postings in the UK and Germany involved the servicing and repair of heavy plant. Then followed a three year period as a Corporal Mechanic, serving with the UN Forces in Cyprus, in control of vehicle and parts acquisition.

Became a Section Commander in (year),
with responsibility for the inspection and
testing of wheeled military vehicles, and for
the control and inspection of work-shop
equipment.
On returning to the UK in (year), the
number of subordinate personnel increased
from five to twenty. Additional
responsibilities included the control and
inspection of a wide variety of high and low
cost items, as well as the repair, maintenance
and testing of wheeled and tracked vehicles.

Certificate of Service reads: Conduct
Exemplary.
Rank on Discharge: Corporal.

Question: *Should a summary be attached where this
approach is made?*

Answer: Yes, when the applicant is still engaged in
the same type of work.

Question: *Might it not be a good idea to present an
Armed Forces career in this way, even if it is
not long and complicated?*

Answer: Yes, but only if it took place some years
previously, and is no longer the main topic.

A STUDENT

Part-time Work Experience

(Year) – *(year)*	Smith's Newsagents 22 Manor Road, Anytown, Midshire
	Morning newspaper round.
(Year)	(Summer holidays) Anytown Leisure Ltd The Promenade, Anytown, Midshire
	Cashier – handing out change to customers.
(Year) – *(year)*	(Weekends) Dot's Cake Shop 14 Belgrave Road, Anytown, Midshire
	Sales Assistant – selling bread and cakes, as well as helping in the bakery.
(Year) – *(year)*	(Weekends and Summer holidays) Anytown Stables Church Road, Anytown, Midshire
	Stable Yard Assistant – grooming, cleaning out and exercising horses.

Additional Information

School:
Prefect.
Captain of Netball Team and member of
Hockey Team.
Duke of Edinburgh Award Scheme
– Silver Award.

University:
Treasurer of the Anytown University Fund
for Distressed Former Students.

OUTSIDE ACTIVITIES

Hobbies   All animals – particularly horses.
              Comic Opera.

References   Available on request.

Question: *Is it not a good idea to enclose copies of
                testimonials or names of referees with each
                application?*

Answer: These are not generally enclosed with the
               CV, but there are exceptions.
                   Students and graduates invariably include
               the names of referees, whether requested to
               do so or not. Professional people with an
               established career often do the same, and I
               am not opposed to this, but remember that
               the final entry on the CV will then read:
                   References – Enclosed.
               Typing the names and addresses of referees
               (usually two, sometimes three), onto a
               separate sheet for photocopying, is
               preferable to including them on the last
               page of the CV, because changing or adding
               one at a later date will not then interfere
               with the CV itself.
                   A minority of people possess written
               testimonials from previous employers.
               Where these are outstanding in their praise
               of an individual's integrity and competence,
               I usually recommend enclosing the best two,
               whatever the person's trade or profession
               might be.

Question: *Unlike earlier examples, the career history
                does not run in reverse, and the exact starting
                and finishing dates are not shown. Why?*

Answer: It can be a good idea for a young person to show clearly that he started work as soon as he was old enough, rather than having waited until he had no choice in the matter.

                  As for starting and finishing dates, obviously the whole working period would be constantly interrupted by academic pursuits.

Question: *Is it wise for someone who might be in the final year of a degree course to admit to having done such jobs?*

Answer: Yes. It is important to display a positive willingness to tackle almost anything.

Question: *Why tell people that you were a school prefect or a games captain?*

Answer: Positions held at school can sometimes influence the reader's attitude, especially where the applicant sees himself as a suitable candidate for a position requiring self-motivation and the ability to shoulder heavy responsibility.

                  To have been a school prefect is an indicator pointing in the right direction. A house captain or captain of a school team, e.g. football, cricket, athletics, netball, etc., indicates a degree of leadership quality. To have been a member of a school team or teams suggests an ability to function in harmony with others.

                  Positions held at university are worthwhile inclusions, provided they do not appear so time consuming that the reader might gain the impression that the applicant has his priorities in the wrong order.

Question: *Why is part-time work not shown in all CVs?*

Answer: When a full-time career has been established, it is likely to overshadow anything that has gone before, although some part-time work may still be worth including, e.g. Territorial Army weekend service. This would come under Outside Activities, as would voluntary work in aid of charity, or perhaps the St John Ambulance Brigade.

Further coverage concerning part-time work will be found on page 109 in Chapter 7, Problems, Problems.

AN ESTATE AGENT

EXPERIENCE/ACHIEVEMENTS

Feb. (year)   Anytown Estates Ltd
– to date   105–107 High Street, Anytown, Midshire
                  – Estate Agents and Valuers (5 branches)

                  September (year) – to date
Branch Manager (Hightown Branch)
responsible to the Financial Director for the
day-to-day running of the branch, with its
high volume Midchester Building Society
agency.
Duties include valuing domestic properties
and securing new business; formulating
press advertisements and property sales
hand-outs; negotiating sales; liaising with
solicitors; attending weekly management
meetings; on-the-job staff training;
interviewing and appointing branch staff
(3).

ACHIEVEMENT: Exceeded (year)
business target by 9.3%, while fees
remained at 2% (firm).

February (year) – September (year)
Valuer/Negotiator (Anytown Branch) –
valuing properties; formulating hand-outs;
negotiating sales; liaising with solicitors;
resolving problems.
Assisted with staff recruitment and
deputised in the Manager's absence.

ACHIEVEMENT: Won a weekend for two
in Paris in (year), for the most improved
performance at any of the five branches.

Apr. (year) Clock Publishing Ltd
– Feb. (year) 41 Cheapside, Anytown, Midshire
   – Media Publishers

   Sales Agent – selling advertising space on
   estate agents' folders to tradesmen and
   retailers.

July (year) H & L Music
– Apr. (year) 169 Church Street, Anytown, Midshire
   – Retailers of Records, Cassettes and
   Compact Discs

   Sales Assistant – selling; display; stock
   control.

OUTSIDE ACTIVITIES

Hobbies Ornithology.
    Water skiing and rock climbing.

Foreign French – passable.
Languages

References Available on request.

Question: *This is the first example in which the
applicant claims to be able to speak a foreign
language, but why say 'passable'?*

Answer: If the applicant is fluent, it should say so on
the CV. If the applicant can just get by, it
will say 'passable'.
  Unless the language in question is spoken
reasonably well, it must not be included.

Question: *Why is the employer's post code never
shown?*

Answer: Few applicants are able to remember the
post codes of past employers.

Question: *What address can I put down if one of my past employers has gone out of business and is no longer there?*

Answer: You are writing a concise account of your career history as it has taken place. The fact that one of your former employers is no longer around is not relevant. The address from which they conducted their business when you worked for them is the address you should use. Alternatively, if they are still in business but have moved to new premises, you could give their current address. This is particularly worthwhile, in the case of a former employer who is likely to give you a favourable recommendation, if approached by a prospective employer.

A REGIONAL SALES MANAGER

EXPERIENCE/ACHIEVEMENTS

Apr. (year) | Flakey Friend Ltd
– to date | 126–132 Elephants Walk, Anytown, Midshire
– Manufacturers and Distributors of Breakfast Cereals

August (year) – to date
Midland Counties Regional Sales Manager responsible to the National Sales Manager, Mr J Jones, for the profitable growth of business throughout the region. Responsibilities cover promotions, distribution and the effective display of products; recruitment and development of sales representatives (8).

ACHIEVEMENT: During this time, a 27% increase in sales (volume) has taken place and sales targets are consistently being exceeded by 3%–5%.

March (year) – August (year)
Area Sales Manager responsible to the Regional Sales Manager for effective space allocation and promotion of the company's products.
Six subordinate sales representatives.

ACHIEVEMENT: Consistently exceeded sales targets, by up to 6%.

April (year) – March (year)
Sales Representative – developing new business throughout the area, and promoting a new product.

ACHIEVEMENT: Awarded an engraved

gold watch, presented by the Managing
Director in person, in recognition of the
success with which the new product had
been launched in the area.

June (year)   Wispy Hair Products Ltd
– Apr. (year)   New Road, Anytown, Midshire

Sales Representative – developing the
company's business through high street
outlets and supermarket chains.

Feb. (year)   The Southern Gas Co
– June (year)   Leigh Road, Anytown, Midshire

Showroom Sales Assistant – selling
domestic gas appliances.

July (year)   Anytown Colourings Ltd
– Feb. (year)   Lowe Road, Anytown, Midshire
                     – Suppliers of Paint and Wallcoverings to
                     the Decorating Trade

Warehouse Assistant – unloading and
stacking incoming stock.

OUTSIDE ACTIVITIES

Hobbies   Squash, tennis and making home movies.
References   Available on request.

Question: *Why, on one occasion, does the applicant
                  give the name of the person to whom he is
                  reporting, as well as his job title?*

Answer: Sometimes, a senior company official will be
                  so well respected within the industry that
                  the mere mention of his name could
                  command attention.

Question: *Why do none of the examples disclose the wage or salary?*

Answer: To state the wage or salary being paid in one's present job can be harmful, if it is too far out of line with that of the post being applied for. The danger with stating the earnings level of previous jobs is that the figures would be historic, and the applicant's fortunes would probably depend on the reader's ability to allow for inflation, during the intervening years.

If the job advertisement requests the detail of your current rate of pay, include this in the introductory letter (see page 117).

Question: *Should I ask a third party to pass an opinion on my CV (and letters) before they are sent out?*

Answer: It is a good idea to let someone have a look even if only to check for spelling mistakes. But danger lurks. The urge to criticise is just one facet of human nature, and the chosen party may not feel happy in returning the documents with little, or no comment. The possible consequences are obvious and potentially destabilising. Try to choose someone whose opinions are worth having, but who is not a close acquaintance. This will minimise the risk of intrusion by the individual's emotions, and make an objective appraisal more likely.

4
THE CAREER HISTORY PART TWO

A collection of career histories from which outside activities and references available have been omitted, in order to avoid tedious repetition. These should, of course, be included when preparing your own CV.

A PLUMBING AND HEATING ENGINEER

EXPERIENCE

Jan. (year) *– to date*	Bates, Barlow (Construction) Ltd Park House, Eagle Industrial Estate Anytown, Midshire – New 1500 bed teaching hospital in Riyadh, Saudi Arabia

Foreman Plumber in charge of twenty expatriate tradesmen and up to forty Filipino labourers.
Responsible for all pipework including medical gas, water, sprinkler and irrigation systems; completion of weekly time and bonus sheets.

Feb. (year) *– Jan. (year)*	Rance Leigh Construction (International) Plc, Hounds Road, Anytown, Midshire – New 300 bedroomed hotel at Dubai, UAE

Foreman Plumber in charge of eight expatriate tradesmen and ten Filipino labourers.

Responsible for the installation of kitchen equipment, en suite bathrooms, garden irrigation and sprinkler systems and all related pipework.

Sept. (year)
– Feb. (year)
Harris Mechanical Services Ltd
Abbey Road, Anytown, Midshire
– Sports Centre and Shopping Precinct in Muscat, Oman

Foreman Plumber in charge of up to fifty expatriate plumbers.
Responsible for the installation of galvanised and copper pipework; PVC underground services; sheet-metal ducting; toilets and showers; irrigation pipework.

Mar. (year)
– Sept. (year)
Hull & Blackwell Ltd
Tower House, Humber Road, Anytown, Midshire
– Industrial Plumbing Contractors
– Cann Chemical Factory in Akassa, Nigeria

Plumber installing pneumatic and stainless-steel instrument pipework; steam pipework; chemical storage tanks.

June (year)
– Mar. (year)
Anytown Plumbing and Heating Ltd
Sidings Road, Anytown, Midshire

Plumber fitting bathrooms and installing pipework on a hotel refurbishment contract. Installing new gas central heating systems and appliances, on conversions of large houses to homes for the elderly.

June (year)
– June (year)
The Park Plumbing and Heating Co Ltd
61–63 Park Road, Anytown, Midshire

Apprentice Plumber (Indentured).

A HAIRDRESSER

EXPERIENCE/ACHIEVEMENT

Oct. (year) *– to date*	The Boulevard Hair Studio 2 The Boulevard, Anytown, Midshire

Senior Stylist supervising four hairdressers, providing a service to clients of all ages. Working eight to ten hours a day, duties include on-the-job staff training; balancing daily takings; banking; security of premises (key holder).

ACHIEVEMENT: During this two year period, the volume of business has increased by 18%, despite strong competition in the locality.

June (year) *– Oct. (year)*	The Salon in the Sun 24 Church Road, Anytown, Midshire

Senior Stylist supervising one hairdresser and two juniors, providing either a traditional or contemporary service. Duties included selling hair products; designing interior and window displays; stock control; security and banking of takings.

Nov. (year) *– June (year)*	Victor's Hair Studio 47 Hillside, Anytown, Midshire – Ladies' and Men's Hairdressing Salon

Stylist in a team of seven, providing a high standard of service to tourists and local business people.

July (year) *– Nov. (year)*	Mobile Hair Stylist visiting clients at home. Built up an established client list of one

hundred and twenty, and gained extensive experience in the products of all major manufacturers.

July (year) Anytown Hair Studio
– July (year) 15 Village Walk, Anytown, Midshire

Apprentice Hairdresser.

A BUTCHER

EXPERIENCE

July (year) *– to date*	M H Johnson & Sons (Butchers) Ltd 28 Abbey Road, Anytown, Midshire – Retail Butchers (168 branches)

Shop Manager (Midchester Branch) responsible to the Area Manager for the day-to-day running of the operation and the profitable growth of business, from sales of fresh carcase meat and cooked meats. Duties include the supervision of a butcher and two sales assistants; on-the-job staff training; completing staff time-sheets; the preparation and presentation of carcase meat; purchasing stock; pricing to achieve set margins; daily cash reconciliation; weekly stock-taking and the preparation of weekly trading reports.

Sept. (year) *– July (year)*	Bennett's 178 High Street, Anytown, Midshire – Wholesale and Retail Butchers, Sausage and Pie Makers

Butcher/Cutter working in a team of five. Duties included cutting meat for display; arranging window and counter displays; preparing cooked meats, i.e. ham, beef, pork, black puddings and barbecued chickens.

July (year) *– Sept. (year)*	R & H Leigh 64 Shaw Road, Anytown, Midshire – Family Butchers

Butcher – cutting up cows, sheep and pigs; boning and rolling meats; ordering carcases,

hams, bacon and fowl; arranging displays;
serving customers.

July (year) F Southworth
– July (year) 95 North Road, Anytown, Midshire
– Retail Butchers, Sausage and Pie Makers

Apprentice Butcher learning all aspects of
the trade, e.g. cutting, boning and rolling;
making sausages, pies, black puddings and
potted meat; quality control; costing and
pricing; display.

A CAR SALESMAN

EXPERIENCE/ACHIEVEMENTS

Aug. (year)
– to date

Anytown Automotive Ltd
23–27 St Patrick's Road, Anytown,
Midshire
– Rover Main Dealers

November (year) – to date
Sales Manager responsible to the Dealer
Principal for achieving agreed minimum
new vehicle sales figures, and complying
with used vehicle sales budgets.
Duties include ordering and control of new
vehicle stocks; meeting customer finance
targets; control and motivation of five sales
staff, four valeters and three office
personnel.

ACHIEVEMENTS: 17% increase in unit
sales of new vehicles in first year; used
vehicle sales consistently ahead of budgets.

August (year) – November (year)
Senior Sales Executive selling new Rover
cars and selected used cars.
Duties included developing the business
user market; used car appraisals; promoting
private and business user funding facilities;
compiling sales staff rotas.

ACHIEVEMENT: 67% unit sales increase
to business users in the first year.

Apr. (year)
– Aug. (year)

Emerson's (Anytown) Ltd
19–23 High Street, Anytown, Midshire
– Mazda Main Dealers

New and Used Car Salesman/
Administrator.

Duties – new and used car sales; used car evaluation; completing finance, insurance and registration documentation; liaison with customer and workshop.

July (year)
– Apr. (year)

J L Jupp (Motors) Ltd
Suffolk Road, Anytown, Midshire
– Lada Main Dealers

Junior Car Salesman learning show-room and office techniques and procedures.

A HEAVY PLANT/CRANE OPERATOR

EXPERIENCE

Oct. (year) *– to date*	ABC Plant Hire Ltd Bridge Street, Anytown, Midshire

Heavy Plant Operator – driving 'dozers, motorscrapers, wheeled shovels and dump trucks in bulk earthwork contracts. Much site reinstatement work.

Sept. (year) *– Oct. (year)*	Ram International plc Willow Road, Anytown, Midshire – Civil Engineering Contractors Motorway Construction Contract

Plant Foreman – liaising with Works Manager; allocation of work to forty drivers operating 'dozers, excavators, loading shovels and dump trucks.

Feb. (year) *– Sept. (year)*	Heave-Ho Ltd Moor Road, Anytown, Midshire – Civil Engineering Contractors Saudi Arabian Airport Contract

Heavy Plant Operator – 'dozing and stockpiling demolition rubble; levelling rock; stripping concealed rock for quarries; levelling fill for runway, apron and roads to finished levels; all reinstatement work.

Nov. (year) *– Feb. (year)*	J J Jones Ltd New Street, Anytown, Midshire – Civil Engineering and Building Contractors Contracted to Libyan Government – constructing a new roadway

Heavy Plant Operator – driving 'dozers and motorscrapers.

Jan. (year)   UK & Foreign Technical Services
– Nov. (year)   Employers Ltd, 122–128 The Square, Anytown, Midshire
Prison Contract for the Nigerian Government

Crane/Plant Operator driving mobile and rough terrain cranes on the construction of steel framed two storey buildings, with concrete panel cladding.
Driving 'dozers, face shovels and motorscrapers.

Sept. (year)   ABS Plant Hire Ltd
– Jan. (year)   Turnbull Road, Garth Industrial Estate, Anytown, Midshire
Cann Oil Refinery Contract

Crane Operator – installation of heavy machinery; movement and location of large capacity vessels; lifting steelwork.

Sept. (year)   Maxisenta (Marine) Ltd
– Sept. (year)   28–34 Dunne Road, Anytown, Midshire
Deep-sea Salvage; Offshore Oil and Gas Exploration.

Crane Operator (Offshore – North Sea) on the 'Maxi Driller'.
Duties – loading and unloading supply vessels; stacking containers; lifting drill floor equipment. Supervised a six man deck crew and all loading and unloading of bulk supplies.

July (year)   Wolfe Bros (Anytown) Ltd
– Sept. (year)   Hyde Road, Anytown, Midshire

– Steel Stockholders

Crane Operator on mobile and overhead cranes.

July (year)   J A Smith (Farms) Ltd
– July (year) Back Lane, Anytown, Midshire

General Farm Worker/Tractor Driver.

A BANK CLERK

EXPERIENCE

Sept. (year) | The Moorland Bank Plc
– to date | St Bartholomew's Road, Hightown, Midshire

April (year) – to date
– Anytown Branch

Administration Clerk (Grade 3) responsible for the effective supervision of seven correspondence clerks. Duties include the control of bid deposits; close checking of suspense account statements; control of foreign transactions; balancing of travellers' cheques; opening and distributing incoming post; assisting with security checks and tests, re: premises and strongroom.

May (year) – April (year)
– Sometown Branch

Administration Clerk (Grade 3) in a team of three, responsible for securities, i.e. the charging of mortgages, life policies, stocks and shares.

June (year) – May (year)
– Moortown Branch

Administration Clerk (Grade 3) – duties similar to Sometown (above), but with frequent relief work. Customers included immigrants with language difficulties, and many business people conducting overseas transactions. Authorised to sanction loan applications up to £1500.

February (year) – June (year)
– Anytown Branch

Administration Clerk (Grade 2) – updating
and balancing the general ledger accounts;
foreign currency exchange; international
payment transfers; counter service.

September (year) – February (year)
– Hightown Branch

Administration Clerk (Grade 1) – computer
terminal input of day's transactions;
updating savings accounts' pass-books;
encoding incoming cheques; dealing with
customer enquiries by telephone and in
person.

A DANCER

EXPERIENCE

July (year)
– Sept. (year)
   Summer Extravaganza
The Hippodrome, Anytown, Midshire
– Musical Comedy Show

Dancing in a duo performing three,
five-minute, routines.

Dec. (year)
– Jan. (year)
   (Christmas Season – six weeks)
The Central Pier Pavilion
Anytown, Midshire
– Mother Goose

Dancing five routines twice daily, in a
troupe of four. Designed costumes; trained
stand-ins; assisted with lighting.

Jan. (year)
– May (year)
   Curtain Call Theatrical Agency
Bourne Road, Anytown, Midshire
– Night Club Contract in Athens

Dancing four, three-minute, solo routines,
five nights a week.

July (year)
– Sept. (year)
   The Harry and Barry Summer Show
Theatre Royal, Anytown, Midshire

Dancing four, five-minute routines, in a
troupe of eight, six nights a week.
Personally choreographed the routines.

June (year)
– Sept. (year)
   The Hotel Sahara Cabaret Bar
East Beach, Anytown, Midshire

Solo Dancer performing four, five-minute,
routines, five nights a week.

| *(Year)* | The Palace Theatre |
| *– (year)* | Anytown, Midshire |

Dancer in five Christmas pantomimes (each running for six weeks), i.e. Dick Whittington; Cinderella; Snow White and the Seven Dwarfs; Aladdin; Babes in the Wood.

Promotional Work

| *(Year)* | The J A Smith Model Agency |
| *– (year)* | 9 West Drive, Anytown, Midshire |

Promotional assignments for swimwear and soft drinks. Milesmaker F701 Sports Car Launch – photographed with the car, and appeared nationally in four motoring magazines.

A POLICEMAN

– seeking work, following retirement from the Police Service.

EXPERIENCE

Aug. (year) Midshire Constabulary
– June (year)

> *November (year) – June (year)*
> – Stationed at Anytown South
>
> Collator (Intelligence Officer) responsible for correlating information; organising conferences; liaising with security personnel from local stores and factories; instructing new recruits in intelligence work.
>
> *April (year) – November (year)*
> – Anytown North
>
> Coroner's Officer responsible to the Chief Superintendent and the Coroner for all administrative procedures, in relation to deaths referred to the Coroner.
> Duties included visiting scenes of reported deaths; taking witness statements; deciding on further police action; liaising with pathologists and solicitors; conducting mortuary identifications; liaising with appropriate police departments and government agencies; collating inquest data; completing sudden death forms.
>
> *January (year) – April (year)*
> – Hightown Central
>
> Duty Officer – handling enquiries and complaints in the public office; writing reports; maintaining records; issuing lost

property receipts; directing car and foot patrols by radio.

October (year) – January (year)
– Midchester Central

Uniformed Constable running the Traffic Wardens' Ticket Office, i.e. issuing notices to recover overdue fines' payments; maintaining records.

February (year) – October (year)
– Midchester South

Uniformed Constable – responding to 999 calls; attending road traffic accidents; dealing with sudden death situations.

August (year) – February (year)
– Hightown South

Uniformed Constable on foot patrol, following completion of ten week course at Home Office training centre.

A FINANCIAL CONSULTANT

EXPERIENCE/ACHIEVEMENTS

Nov. (year) Anytown Financial Services Ltd
– to date London Street, Anytown, Midshire

Financial Consultant visiting potential
clients, identifying client needs and advising
on life assurance, pensions and investments.

ACHIEVEMENT: Expanded the client
base by 57% in the first year.

Feb. (year) Eternal Life Assurance Ltd
– Nov. (year) 78–82 High Street, Anytown, Midshire

Area Representative (Hightown)
responsible for selling life assurance,
personal pensions, company pension plans,
investment packages and endowment
mortages.

ACHIEVEMENT: Never lower than third
in the monthly sales table of thirty-six area
representatives.

Aug. (year) K E Tagg Associates
– Feb. (year) 21 Leicester Road, Anytown, Midshire
– Insurance Brokers

Client Adviser – dealing with all aspects of
property and motor insurance, i.e.
supplying quotations; amending policies;
processing claims; updating files; preparing
accounts.

Apr. (year) Highgate Developments (Anytown) Ltd
– Aug. (year) Greenacres Road, Anytown, Midshire
– House Builders

Sales Negotiator – conducting show house
viewings; advising on fixtures and fittings;
selling sites; liaising with site agent,
company's solicitor and vendor's solicitor.

July (year)   Anytown Estates
– Apr. (year) 105–107 High Street, Anytown, Midshire

Clerk/Receptionist.

A SCAFFOLDER

EXPERIENCE

Jan. (year)
– to date

MASS Offshore Ltd
Steele Road, Anytown, Midshire

Foreman Scaffolder (Offshore – North Sea) on Cann Oil Platform.
Duties – supervising up to thirty scaffolders; assessing jobs and ordering materials; liaising with electricians, riggers and painters; quality control; working to drawings and stress limits; ensuring compliance with health and safety at work regulations; acquiring work permits; completing staff time-sheets and keeping the safety standards book.

Mar. (year)
– Dec. (year)

Rance Leigh Construction (International) Plc, Hounds Road, Anytown, Midshire
– Norsham Nuclear Power Station (Stage II)

Advanced Scaffolder erecting all types of scaffolding, up to 180 ft high.

Aug. (year)
– Mar. (year)

Standfast Scaffolding Ltd
19 Halls Lane, Anytown, Midshire

December (year) – March (year)
– Cann Chemical Plant Maintenance Contract

Advanced Scaffolder working in a team of four, erecting tower and independent scaffolding.

August (year) – December (year)
– Fox 'C' Nuclear Power Station Contract

Advanced Scaffolder erecting suspended
scaffolding inside boilers.

May (year)   RLS (Anytown) Ltd
– Aug. (year)   181 London Road, Anytown, Midshire
                  – Scaffolding Contractors
                  – Oil Rig Rebuilding Contract – UK and
                  Holland

                  Scaffolder working in dry dock, erecting
                  dropping scaffolds and specially designed
                  double fitting hangers.

Mar. (year)   A & J Scaffolding Ltd
– May (year)   34 Gorse Road, Anytown, Midshire

                  Scaffolder on major civil engineering and
                  building works for retail store groups,
                  aircraft manufacturers, banks and churches.

Oct (year)   Anytown Scaffolding Ltd
– Mar. (year)   Back Commercial Street, Anytown,
                  Midshire

                  Scaffolder on theatre and factory
                  maintenance contracts, including a fire
                  damaged 150 bedroomed hotel – erected
                  wall scaffold to cantilevers.

July (year)   Maxisenta Support Services Ltd
– Oct. (year)   36 Dunne Road, Anytown, Midshire
                  – Scaffolding Contractors

                  July (year) – October (year)
                  Scaffolder.

                  July (year) – July (year)
                  Trainee Scaffolder.

A TEACHER

EXPERIENCE

Sept. (year) *– to date*	St Augustine's High School Anytown, Midshire

English Teacher responsible for taking
GCSE and 'A' Level classes.
'A' Level pass rates have exceeded 75%.
Deputised for the Head of Department, for
one term, during his absence.
Appointed Housemistress in September
(year), in charge of 150 children.

Sept. (year) *– July (year)*	Anytown School Anytown, Midshire – Independent Co-Educational School – (Entrance by examination)

English Teacher responsible for teaching
fourth and fifth year classes.
Placed in charge of school debating society
(three to four topical debates each term,
frequently involving other schools).
Drama – supervised two major productions
each year.
Arranged and accompanied educational
trips to Holland and Germany.

Sept. (year) *– July (year)*	Anyborough Comprehensive School Anyborough, Midshire

English Teacher taking classes to 'O' Level
standard.
Extra curricular duties included adapting
and directing productions for the school
dramatic society.

Sept. (year)   Anytown High School
– July (year)   Anytown, Midshire
                  – (Now closed and formerly Anytown
                  Grammar School)

                  English Teacher taking English classes up to
                  'O' Level standard.
                  Actively involved in the introduction of
                  Integrated Humanities.

A MARINE ENGINEER

– seeking work on or offshore.

EXPERIENCE

Sept. (year)   MPD Ships Ltd
– to date   93–99 Wharfe Street, Anytown, Midshire
                 – General Cargo Ships

October (year) – to date
Second Engineer Officer responsible for the
implementation of a planned maintenance
programme, for the main propulsion
engines and auxiliary power sources.
Responsibilities include being in charge of
the watch (8 hours), and supervising the
repair and routine maintenance of
refrigeration, air conditioning, water
desalination and oil purification systems.

September (year) – October (year)
Third Engineer Officer responsible for
carrying out weekly tests of Unmanned
Machinery Space alarm systems; repair and
routine maintenance of the electric steering
motors and the diesel powered electricity
generators.

Aug. (year)   Tank and Container Marine Freighters Ltd
– Sept. (year) 41–43 Dock Road, Anytown, Midshire
                 – Crude Oil Tankers and Container Ships

June (year) – September (year)
Fourth Engineer Officer in charge of the
watch.
Responsible for the repair and routine
maintenance of compressors, oil
purification centrifuges, pumps and related
systems.

August (year) – June (year)
Junior Engineer in charge of the auxiliary systems watch.

Aug. (year) – Aug. (year)   Global Tankers Ltd
231–233 Flag Road, Anytown, Midshire – Crude Oil Tankers

Indentured Apprentice Marine Engineer (Cadet).

Summary   Extensive experience gained with:

Low and medium speed, 2 and 4 stroke diesel engines up to 30,000 bhp.
Diesel powered generators up to 1,500 kW.
Low-pressure water tube boilers and related water treatment processes.
Water desalination.
Oil purification.
Refrigeration and air conditioning.
Hydraulic systems up to 2,000 PSI working pressure.
Air compressors.
Centrifugal and screw pumps.
Milling and turning.
Gas and arc welding.

A MANAGING DIRECTOR

EXPERIENCE/ACHIEVEMENTS

Mar. (year)   Baldwin, Barker & Co (Anytown) Ltd
– to date   86 Tower Gate, Anytown, Midshire
           – Property Investment and Development

           July (year) – to date
           Managing Director responsible to the
           Chairman for instant decision making and
           the day-to-day running of the company;
           liaising with company architects, solicitors,
           accountants and bankers, in the planning
           and execution of developments, up to £3.5
           million.
           Responsibilities include scrutinising main
           contractors' returned tender documents and
           presiding at high-level meetings.
           Regular liaison with co-directors covering
           sales, purchases and leases.

           ACHIEVEMENT: Through encouraging
           an improved performance from existing
           staff members and recruiting highly
           motivated executives of proven ability,
           company turnover increased by 35% within
           two years.
           Despite adverse market forces, the level of
           activity has been maintained with
           corresponding profitability. Recently
           rewarded by the company with a Porsche.

           September (year) – July (year)
           Director of Purchasing and Development
           responsible to the Managing Director for
           researching proposed development and
           redevelopment projects, i.e. ensuring cost-
           effectiveness, long-term viability, or quick
           resale profit potential; obtaining engineers'

soil test reports; negotiating the purchase of greenfield sites and existing buildings, e.g. office-blocks, factories and warehouses; liaising with all relevant professions.

ACHIEVEMENT: Personally responsible for negotiating the purchase of a partially completed £800,000 development from the Moorland Bank. This development was subsequently completed and sold, with a net profit to the company of £240,000.

March (year) – September (year)
Buyer/Negotiator responsible for travelling throughout the UK, negotiating options on agricultural land, as well as purchasing land with outline planning permission. Required to liaise with architects and chief planning officers, and participate in the presentation of planning applications.
Fought and won an appeal to the DOE over the refusal of planning permission to build a new office-block.
Four subordinate head office personnel.

Feb. (year) – Mar. (year)   Midshire Estates Ltd
122–124 Clifton Road, Anytown, Midshire – Estate Agents, Auctioneers and Valuers (30 branches)

Branch Manager (Midchester) responsible to the Managing Director for the efficient day-to-day running of the branch, i.e. securing instructions to sell house properties; preparing valuations, newspaper advertisements and property fact sheets; negotiating sales; advising purchasers with regard to mortgage facilities; liaising with clients' solicitors.

Two subordinate negotiators, six full and
part-time administrative and clerical staff.

Aug. (year)   Anytown Building Society
– Jan. (year)   188 New Road, Anytown, Midshire
                  – 400 branches

January (year) – January (year)
Assistant Manager (North End Branch).

August (year) – January (year)
Administrative Clerk/Cashier (Midchester
Branch).

5
COMPLETE CVS

A JOINER

PERSONAL DETAILS

Full Name:	George Donkin
Address:	14 Westbourne Road, Anytown, Midshire, XX1 1YY
Telephone No:	Anytown (01888) 888888
Date of Birth:	28th February (year)
Place of Birth:	Anytown, Midshire
Nationality:	British
Marital Status:	Married with son aged 15 and daughter aged 12
Driving Licence:	Current (full)
Passport No:	X 888888Y – expires August (year)

CURRICULUM VITAE

EDUCATION AND QUALIFICATIONS

Sept. (year) – July (year)   Anytown Comprehensive School
Anytown, Midshire

June (year)	*CSE*	
Woodwork		(1)
Art		(1)
Engineering Drawing		(2)
Mathematics		(3)
English		(3)
History		(4)

Sept. (year)	Anytown College of Further and Higher
– June (year)	Education
	– Day Release and Evening Classes

June (year)
City and Guilds of London Institute
Craft Certificate – Carpentry and Joinery

EXPERIENCE

Feb. (year)	F Lynch & Son Ltd
– to date	217 Beacon Road, Garth Industrial Estate, Anytown, Midshire
	– Builders, Shopfitters and Bar Fitters

Foreman Joiner on a £5m club refit and extension. Responsible for the supervision of thirty-eight joiners, plumbers, electricians, bricklayers and labourers engaged in the construction of period bars, static and revolving stages, all backstage facilities and a restaurant.

| Oct. (year) | J S Rigg (Builders) Ltd |
| – Feb. (year) | 45 Aqueduct Street, Anytown, Midshire |

Foreman Joiner – supervision of twenty joiners on the rebuilding of a 300 bedroom, 4 star hotel, damaged by fire: bars; studdings; spiral staircases; hardwood dance floors; door casings.

Nov. (year)	H P Construction and Design Ltd
– Oct. (year)	106–108 Victoria Road, Anytown, Midshire
	– Public House and Hotel Refurbishment Contractors

Joiner in the workshop making bars, back-fittings, door casings and mock period

	timber beams. Worked on site – fixing false ceilings and raised areas.
Mar. (year) *– Nov. (year)*	E F Wall & Sons Ltd 81–83 Clay Street, Anytown, Midshire – Building Contractors Joiner – first, second and final fix on new houses.
Nov. (year) *– Mar. (year)*	Oak Tree Joinery 28–30 Coronation Road, Anytown, Midshire – Manufacturers of Replacement Doors and Windows Bench Hand/Installer making and fitting uPVC windows and doors.
July (year) *– Nov. (year)*	Joseph Yorke & Co Ltd 35 Oak Road, Anytown, Midshire – Building Contractors *July (year) – November (year)* Joiner – first, second and final fix on an exclusive housing development. *July (year) – July (year)* Apprentice Joiner (Indentured) – two years in the joinery shop; two years supervised on-the-job training.

OUTSIDE ACTIVITIES

Hobbies	Playing squash, family activities and reading.
References	Available on request.

A RETAIL SALES MANAGER

PERSONAL DETAILS

Full Name:	James Smith
Address:	8 Ashburton Close, Anytown, Midshire, XX1 1YY
Telephone No:	Anytown (01888) 888888
Date of Birth:	19th July (year)
Place of Birth:	Anytown, Midshire
Nationality:	British
Marital Status:	Married – no children
Driving Licence:	Current (clean)

CURRICULUM VITAE

EDUCATION AND QUALIFICATIONS

Sept. (year) St George's High School
– July (year) Anytown, Midshire

June (year)   GCE 'O' Level
Mathematics   (A)
English Language   (B)
History   (B)
Geography   (B)
Physics   (C)
Chemistry   (C)
Biology   (C)
English Literature (C)

June (year)   GCE 'A' Level
Mathematics   (B)
History   (D)

TRAINING

Fashionwear Shops plc

Feb. (year)	Training the Trainer	(1 week)
Oct. (year)	Staff Appraisal	(2 days)
July (year)	Man Management/Leadership	(2 days)
May (year)	Computerised Stock Control	(2 days)
Oct. (year)	Motivating the Customer	(1 day)

EXPERIENCE/ACHIEVEMENTS

Oct. (year)
– to date
Fashionwear Shops Plc
121–129 Arcadia Road, Anytown, Midshire
– 372 branches nationwide

January (year) – to date
General Manager (Midchester) responsible
to the Area Manager for meeting sales
budgets and controlling the expenditure
budget to set parameters.
Duties include development of sales staff;
conducting weekly staff meetings; attending
monthly management meetings; cost control
(including cleaning and maintenance);
presentation and display; stock control;
ensuring compliance with health and safety
at work legislation.

ACHIEVEMENT: 12% increase in
business turnover in first full financial year.

October (year) – January (year)
Assistant Manager (Northend) responsible
for the training and motivation of sales staff
(10) using EPOS; completing staff time-
sheets and appraisals; stock control; security
of cash and premises (key holder);
presentation and display.

Nov. (year) *– Oct. (year)*	Kelly & Smart Ltd 71–75 Burlingham Road, Anytown, Midshire

– Ladies' and Gents' Fashions (5 branches)

Manager (Anytown) responsible to the Financial Director for the day-to-day running of the business. Duties included recruitment and training of staff (5); designing window and interior displays; formulating and placing local advertisements; balancing daily takings; banking; submitting a weekly trading analysis; security (key holder).

ACHIEVEMENT: Consistently exceeded agreed budgets, despite a strong presence from three similar retail shops within a distance of five hundred metres.

July (year) *– Nov. (year)*	Simm's Ltd 44–52 Henry Street, Anytown, Midshire – Departmental Store (80 branches)

Floor Supervisor (Children's Wear) – security of stock and cash; daily balancing of tills; float provision; dealing with complaints; ensuring compliance with regulations.

July (year) *– July (year)*	King's Menswear 18–20 Underdown Road, Anytown, Midshire – (Established in 1868)

January (year) – July (year)
Sales Assistant.

July (year) – January (year)
Sales Trainee.

OUTSIDE ACTIVITIES

Hobbies	Swimming, snooker, cycling and watching football.
References	Available on request.

A NURSE

PERSONAL DETAILS

Full Name: Brenda Ann Jones RGN
UKCC PIN No: 00Z0000X
Address: 84 Agnew Road, Anytown,
                    Midshire, XX1 1YY
Telephone No: Anytown (01888) 888888
Date of Birth: 21st July (year)
Place of Birth: Anytown, Midshire
Nationality: British
Marital Status: Single
Driving Licence: Current (clean)

CURRICULUM VITAE

EDUCATION AND QUALIFICATIONS

Sept. (year)   Anytown High School
– July (year)   Anytown, Midshire

                  June (year)   GCE 'O' Level
                  Mathematics   (B)
                  English Language   (B)
                  English Literature   (B)
                  Geography   (C)
                  Physics   (C)
                  Biology   (C)

                  June (year)   GCE 'A' Level
                  Mathematics with
                     Statistics   (D)
                  Psychology   (E)

Sept. (year)   The Royal Albert Memorial Hospital
– Nov. (year)   School of Nursing
                  November (year)   RGN qualified

TRAINING

Jan. (year)	Assessor's Course	(2 days)
Aug. (year)	First Line Management	(4 days)
Mar. (year)	Lifting and Handling	(1 day)
June (year)	Intensive Care	(1 week)
Nov. (year)	HIV/Drugs Misuse	(2 days)

Professional Association

Member of the Royal College of Nursing

EXPERIENCE

Feb. (year)
– to date
Anytown Royal Hospital
Redwing Road, Anytown, Midshire

September (year) – to date
Staff Nurse (Grade E) on night duty in the Acute General Surgical Ward (38 beds). Duties include dealing with massive injury patients needing emergency surgery; major abdominal surgical cases and patients with peripheral vascular disease. Supervising and teaching student nurses; liaising with medical and paramedical staff.

February (year) – September (year)
Staff Nurse (Grade D) on the Acute Male Medical Ward (25 beds).
Many tracheostomy and ventilated patients, and terminally ill patients with cardiac problems. Empathised with anxious and bereaved relatives.

Sept. (year)
– Feb. (year)
The Royal Albert Memorial Hospital
Anytown, Midshire

November (year) – February (year)
Staff Nurse (Grade D) on the Elderly
Persons' Rehabilitation Ward (23 beds).
Duties – medicine rounds; pressure sore
prevention; use of preventative medicine;
supervising rehabilitation exercises; liaising
with the multi-disciplinary team.

September (year) – November (year)
Student Nurse – ward based learning
comprised a series of fourteen, eight-week,
placements, i.e.: Acute General; Male
Medical; Female Medical; Male Surgical;
Female Surgical; Geriatric; Community;
Obstetric; Paediatric; Psychiatric; ENT;
Maternity; A & E; Orthopaedic.

OUTSIDE ACTIVITIES

Hobbies   Walking, swimming and foreign travel.

References   Available on request.

A CHEF

PERSONAL DETAILS

Full Name:	Roland Geoffrey Tillotson
Address:	17 Abercrombie Road, Anytown, Midshire, XX1 1YY
Telephone No:	Anytown (01888) 888888
Date of Birth:	5th September (year)
Place of Birth:	Anytown, Midshire
Nationality:	British
Religion:	Christian
Marital Status:	Single
Next of Kin:	Mr & Mrs D G Tillotson (Parents) – address as above.
Driving Licence:	Current (clean)
Passport No:	X 888888Y – expires September (year)
Health:	Excellent

CURRICULUM VITAE

EDUCATION AND QUALIFICATIONS

Sept. (year) – July (year)	The Oaks School Anytown, Midshire

June (year)	*CSE*	
Mathematics		(2)
English		(2)
French		(2)
Geography		(3)
Engineering Drawing		(3)

Sept. (year) – June (year)	Anytown College of Further and Higher Education – Full-time

City and Guilds of London Institute
Certificates
June (year)   706/1 (2 passes)
June (year)   706/2 (1 Credit; 2 Passes)

Royal Society of Arts
June (year)   Catering French   (Pass)

Royal Institute of Public Health and Hygiene
June (year)   The Food Hygiene and
Handling Certificate

EXPERIENCE

Feb. (year)   The Kite Inn
– to date   Honeypot Lane, Anytown, Midshire
                   – Public House
                   – À la carte restaurant (85 covers); hot bar
                   meals

                   Chef preparing up to one hundred and thirty
                   à la carte meals daily, plus one hundred to
                   one hundred and twenty lunch-time and
                   evening bar meals.
                   Control of a second chef, a commis chef and
                   two kitchen assistants; menu planning and
                   costing (56% margin); purchasing stock;
                   hygiene.

Sept. (year)   Anytown Craft and Management
– Feb. (year)   Recruitment Ltd
                   93 Shipley Street, Anytown, Midshire
                   – Saudi Arabian Construction Site

                   Catering Manager responsible to the UK
                   based General Manager for setting up and
                   running a camp for fifteen hundred
                   construction workers.

Responsible for the provision of all meals; stock control; planning and costing; training and motivation of one hundred and twenty catering staff.

Mar. (year)   The Mile End Hotel
– Sept. (year)   122–128 South Promenade, Anytown, Midshire
– 3 Star (65 en suite bedrooms)

Chef – provision of à la carte meals to the restaurant (120 covers); the dining-room (130 covers); two functions rooms.
Provision of takeaway meals and bar snacks.
Control of a second chef, four commis chefs and three kitchen assistants.

Apr. (year)   Anytown Holiday Centre Ltd
– Mar. (year)   Beach Road, Anytown, Midshire
– Holiday Camp

Chef – control of seven cooks and five kitchen assistants, preparing two thousand plus fast-food meals daily.

Jan. (year)   University of Anytown
– Apr. (year)   Seafield Road, Anytown, Midshire

Commis Chef (one of six) involved in the preparation of one thousand plus cafeteria meals daily, on a three week menu cycle.

Apr. (year)   The Bird Cage Restaurant
– Jan. (year)   Anytown, Midshire
– Anglo-French Restaurant (65 covers)

Commis Chef making croissants; soups; cakes and rolls; sorbets.

Aug. (year)   The Middle West Hotels Group
– Apr. (year)   Anytown, Midshire
                  – 3 and 4 Star Hotels

                  Commis Chef moving between the
                  company's six hotels.

Aug. (year)   The Fiddler's Arms
– Aug. (year)   Green Lane, Anytown, Midshire
                  – High-class Grill-Room Restaurant (60
                  covers)

                  Trainee Chef.

OUTSIDE ACTIVITIES

Hobbies   Sea fishing and cycling.

References   Available on request.

6
THE WRONG WAY TO WRITE YOUR OWN CV

– followed by a table of questions and answers.

Name: Michelle Brown   Address: 85 New Road,
Date of Birth: 28th March (year)   Anytown,
Marital Status: Single   Midshire,
Children: Darren – born 6th July (year)   XX1 1YY
        Chantelle – born 2nd May (year)
Driving Licence: Yes

Education, Qualifications and Training

        Anytown High School (5 years)
        Anytown College of Further and Higher
        Education (2 years)

        Qualifications – 6 GCSE subjects
           RSA Word Processing Certificate

Work Experience

        With having to take care of my children, I
have not had a full-time job since leaving
college. Darren is now at school, and my
mum looks after him in the holidays.
Chantelle has started at nursery school and
my boyfriend's mum takes her and picks her
up, so I am now looking for a job.

        I had a full-time job with Day, Knight & Co,
Chartered Accountants, 8 Water Street,

Anytown, and went to college in the evenings. But I had to leave Day, Knight & Co, to have Darren.

I started work as an Office Junior. Then they advertised for a Typist/Receptionist. I applied and I was given the position. I was more or less in charge of the office, until I left to have Darren.

Since Darren was born, I have worked three evenings a week as a Barmaid at the Dog and Partridge Inn, Ball Street, Anytown. I had two months off when Chantelle was born, but they took me on again because they said I was so good at the job.

During my last year at school, I was a Shelf Stocker at Anytown Supermarket. This helped me to develop an understanding of the work ethic and enabled me to enhance my interpersonal skills.

Hobbies and Interests

My hobbies are children, playing video games and socialising.

Question: *What is wrong with this CV?*

Answer: Just about everything. To begin with, the personal details appear to have been thrown at the paper, and then allowed to remain at the point of impact. The reader's eyes will be darting from side to side across the page, in a frantic search for information. The need to offer a presentation which is easy for the eye to scan down is clearly illustrated here. Equally important, is the selective use of underlining (or italics) which is non-existent in this example.

If the reader proves sufficiently determined to arrive at education, qualifications and training, he will find himself wondering about things like: GCSE subjects and grades of passes; day release or evening classes; starting and finishing dates.

It may be that the reader is the type who scans the career history first, in which case, the early sections will be of no interest to him, because the CV will go straight into the waste-bin.

Question: *Can you tell me which was her most recent job?*

Answer: Since Chantelle is the younger of her two children, and Chantelle's birth is given as the reason for her temporary absence from the Dog and Partridge, I would say that the second job was her most recent. But don't think about it too long, or you will soon be as muddle headed as she is.

Question: *She does seem a bit confused, doesn't she?*

Answer: The confusion is caused by her failure to think about what she was doing beforehand, in order to get a clear outline plan of what she was trying to convey. Instead, she has simply spilled the contents of her mind onto the paper, resulting in a composition which tells us at least as much about Dàrren and Chantelle, as it does about her work.

Even more off-putting is the obviously high opinion she has of herself, e.g. 'they took me on again because they said I was so good at the job'. When referring to her job change at Day, Knight & Co, she says, 'I applied and I was given the position'. These smug statements highlight the danger of using the first person singular (I). She goes on to compound her folly by saying 'I was more or less in charge of the office, until I left to have Darren'. Not only will vague statements of this kind fail to impress the reader, they will positively discourage him. Furthermore, in this instance he will have cause for serious doubts about the truth of what she is saying, because no self-respecting firm of chartered accountants would put someone like her in charge of the office.

Question: *What does she mean when she says of her job at the supermarket that 'This helped me to develop an understanding of the work ethic and enabled me to enhance my interpersonal skills'?*

Answer: I most emphatically believe that she does not have the remotest idea what she means. She must have read it somewhere and thought it looked good.

What it means to me is that her career has passed its peak, and that she should resign herself to another forty years at the Dog and Partridge.

Question: *Do you think that having two young children will make it more difficult for her to get a full-time job?*

Answer: Yes, especially so in this case where she makes it very clear that because her children are so important to her, they should be of equal interest to the reader of the CV. The truth is that his interest in her children will not go beyond seeing them as a possible

obstacle to her time-keeping and regular
attendance at work. She has unwittingly
made sure that this fear will occur to him.

There is no need to put children's names
in the CV either.

Question: *Do you think that socialising is a wise thing
to put down as an interest?*

Answer: In this case no. But we all know people who
genuinely like going around meeting others.
There is no harm in saying this, provided
there are two or three other solid leisure
pursuits to place ahead of socialising.

Question: *Why do you consider it unwise for this
applicant to include socialising as an interest?*

Answer: Because her only other interest, besides her
children, is playing video games.

If I were the person reading this CV and
had bothered to read this far, I would guess
that she probably spends an excessive
amount of time on the other side of the bar
at the Dog and Partridge. This is the wrong
impression to give in a CV, since the reader
might easily create an entirely false image of
a bleary eyed, rolling drunkard, stumbling
through the office door every morning two
hours late.

Question: *Should she not have mentioned references?*

Answer: Yes, if she is able to provide them.

7
PROBLEMS, PROBLEMS

Question: *The way the career histories are presented in this book might be all right for most people, but what about someone like me? I am a Fitter/Welder with twenty-three years' experience, working on short-term contracts for so many companies that I lost count years ago.*

Answer: I do not claim that the career histories shown on the preceding pages are the only way of presenting your experience. But I do believe that they represent the best approach for someone writing their own CV, and probably doing it seriously for the first time. However, in this particular instance, I agree that using my chosen format would give rise to a long, over repetitive and tedious read, with negative results being a near certainty. So here we go with something tailored to this problem:

A FITTER/WELDER

Experience   *Large Bore Piling Contracts* – MMA, MIG and TIG.

Piling for tunnel retaining walls, wing and push walls; reinforcing cages; bridge supports; retaining walls for multi-storey hotels, flats and car parks; piling for sewers.

Manufacture – MMA, MIG and TIG to Lloyds standards.

Tanks, chutes and pressure vessels; steam, gas and petrochemical pipework, including carbon and stainless-steel overhead pipes; welding of angle and channel iron support brackets; small bore stainless-steel pipes (½″); stainless-steel ducting.

General

Welding coffer-dams.
Tacking and welding carbon steel.
Cutting out damaged hull sections on general cargo ships, using oxy-propane cutting equipment.
Using oxyacetylene in the repair of deck fittings.
Fitting out boiler houses and associated plant, to drawings and specifications and to Lloyds' standards.
Hospital installation of steam, gas and hot water systems.
Hospital installation of heating and ventilating systems; welding pipework in service ducts.
Fitting, welding and erecting sprinkler systems.
Installing heater batteries and thermostatic valves.
Installing chemical refrigeration plant.
Supervising teams of skilled tradesmen.
Liaising with all trades.

Principal Employers – last ten years to date

Bucholtz Foundations (UK) Ltd, Anytown – Piling Contractors.

Bunn & Bateson Ltd, Anytown
– Heavy Engineering.

Bayland Piling (Anytown) Ltd.

Maxisenta Mechanical Services Ltd,
Anytown.

L F Marsh (Anytown) Ltd
– Heating and Ventilation Contractors.

SGE Fabricators Ltd, Anytown.

Bray Bros Ltd, Anytown
– Civil Engineering.

Jupiter Engineering Ltd, Anytown.

Rutter Welding (Anytown) Ltd
– Structural Engineers.

Spark Engineering Ltd, Anytown.

Britt Site Services Ltd, Anytown
– Fabrication Contractors.

Although the career histories of skilled
tradesmen in the same field are never
exactly alike, the above mix will resemble
what could be expected in this situation. By
putting principal employers as a sub-
heading, we are in effect saying, 'I can't
remember them all, but these are the main
ones'.

   In preparing the career history like this, I
would expect the completed CV to be on
three A4 pages, allowing for an average
take-up of space by the education,
qualifications and training. If space was
available, it would be worthwhile inserting
one or two contracts immediately below
each of the employers listed, e.g.:

Bucholtz Foundations (UK) Ltd, Anytown
– Piling Contractors.

M6 motorway bridge widening.
DSS multi-storey office-block.

Question: *Why not do all CVs this way?*

Answer: I much prefer to match the experience to the
employer or employers, with whom the
particular area of experience was gained.
The above example is a compromise, made
necessary in order to get round a difficult
situation.

Question: *My problem is that I have been pursuing two
distinctly different careers. I have worked for
some employers as a Chauffeur and for
others as an Accounts Clerk. I was told to do
a separate CV for each occupation, but then I
was left with huge unexplained time gaps. If
I put it all on one CV to avoid these gaps, it
looks a bit ridiculous, so what can I do?*

Answer: This is what I call 'two for the price of one',
meaning that when someone in this situation
asks me to prepare their CV, I have no
choice but to do two CVs for the price of
one. Fortunately, it does not happen too
often.
    It is simply a matter of including both
occupations in each CV, in a way which
brings only one of them to the fore. In the
first of the two examples below, the chauffeur
is the prominent one, the accounts clerk
being used only to fill the dreaded gaps. In
the second example, the roles are reversed.

A CHAUFFEUR

EXPERIENCE

Oct. (year)
– to date

Madewell Plastics (Anytown) Ltd
Hove Road, Garth Industrial Estate,
Anytown, Midshire

Chauffeur to the Managing Director, Mr F
P Glynn – driving a Rolls-Royce fifty
thousand miles a year on business trips
throughout England and Scotland. Much
driving in Central London and other major
cities; extensive weekend and late night
work; airport collection of business
executives from overseas.

July (year)
– Oct. (year)

Day, Knight & Co, Chartered Accountants
8 Water Street, Anytown, Midshire

Audit Clerk.

Apr. (year)
–July (year)

Colonel A B Bowman-Smith
The Birches, Forest Road, Anytown,
Midshire
– Lord Lieutenant of Midshire

Chauffeur driving a Rolls-Royce to official
functions, and on holiday journeys to
Switzerland and the South of France.
Duties included driving shooting parties
around the Colonel's country estate in a
Range Rover, and helping the gamekeeper
to recruit beaters.

Nov. (year)
– Apr. (year)

Anytown Sports and Leisure Ltd
1–7 Victory Road, Anytown, Midshire

Accounts Clerk.

Jan. (year)   Mr Joe Yorke – London, Paris, Los Angeles
– Nov. (year)   – Stage and Screen Actor

Chauffeur in UK, France and the USA –
driving Rolls-Royce, Ferrari, Mercedes-
Benz, BMW and Porsche cars.

Aug. (year)   R & L Slack Ltd
– Jan. (year)   68–70 Avenue Road, Anytown, Midshire
– Plumbers' Merchants

Accounts and Administration Clerk.

Mar. (year)   Maxisenta Motor Traction Co Ltd
– Aug. (year)   25–33 Dunne Road, Anytown, Midshire
– Luxury Coach Operators (45 coaches)

Driver – UK and European holiday tours,
e.g. France, Switzerland, Italy, Germany
and Austria.

June (year)   H B Household Appliances Ltd
– Mar. (year)   28–30 Shore Road, Anytown, Midshire

Clerk/Cashier.

AN ACCOUNTS CLERK

EXPERIENCE

Oct. (year)   Madewell Plastics (Anytown) Ltd
– to date   Hove Road, Garth Industrial Estate,
Anytown, Midshire

Chauffeur to the Managing Director.

July (year)   Day, Knight & Co, Chartered Accountants
– Oct. (year)   8 Water Street, Anytown, Midshire

Audit Clerk – preparing trading and
profit and loss accounts for small traders

and partnerships; keeping VAT records and
preparing returns; calculating PAYE and
national insurance.

Apr. (year)   Colonel A B Bowman-Smith
– July (year) The Birches, Forest Road, Anytown,
Midshire
– Lord Lieutenant of Midshire

Chauffeur.

Nov. (year)   Anytown Sports and Leisure Ltd
– Apr. (year) 1–7 Victory Road, Anytown, Midshire

Accounts Clerk – computer input of takings
from squash and badminton courts, bowling
alleys, games machines and vending
machines.
Duties included liaison with all departments
to correct errors; production of weekly cash
sheets; banking.

Jan. (year)   Mr Joe Yorke – London, Paris, Los Angeles
– Nov. (year) – Stage and Screen Actor

Chauffeur.

Aug. (year)   R & L Slack Ltd
– Jan. (year) 68–70 Avenue Road, Anytown, Midshire
– Plumbers' Merchants

Accounts and Administration Clerk –
computer input; preparing sales invoices;
verifying purchase invoices; producing
monthly sales and stock sheets; dealing with
telephone enquiries.

Mar. (year)   Maxisenta Motor Traction Co Ltd
– Aug. (year) 25–33 Dunne Road, Anytown, Midshire

    – Luxury Coach Operators

Driver.

June (year)   H B Household Appliances Ltd
– Mar. (year) 28–30 Shore Road, Anytown, Midshire

Clerk/Cashier – keeping sales and purchase ledgers; typing materials orders; computer input of stock data; checking incoming delivery documentation; reconciling cash with till rolls.

Question: *The career history examples do not appear to offer much help to the self-employed. Should they approach the writing of their CVs in the same way as everyone else?*

Answer: The self-employed generally fall into one of two categories.

The first, and perhaps more common, is tradesmen or salesmen working on an hourly or commission basis. Apart from reduced protection under the law, the main difference between this type of self-employment and employee status lies in the method of payment. Duties and responsibilities, time-keeping and the standard of work requirements will not necessarily differ to a large extent. Therefore, the CV will be presented in the usual way.

The second category includes those who have been self-employed running their own business. While some prospective employers may be discouraged, by the possibility that these applicants might not conform easily to the disciplines of full-time employment, others will be aware that the customer is the most demanding master of all.

If long hours in excess of the accepted norm have been worked, week in and week out, this fact should be conveyed, as in the following career history:

Aug. (year)   J Smith (Building Contractor)
– to date   Lower Lane, Anytown, Midshire
           – New House Building; Extensions; Home Improvements etc.

Proprietor – totally responsible for running the business with up to six skilled tradesmen and ten labourers.
Working an average of sixty-five hours a week, responsibilities include purchasing materials; staff recruitment, motivation and control; preparation of tenders; book-keeping and VAT returns; liaising with all associated professions.
Four contracts, each exceeding £200,000 in value, have been successfully completed during the last three years.

Question: *Would a prospective employer not wonder why the business was not continuing?*

Answer: Possibly. Therefore the applicant might make the following inclusion in an accompanying letter:

Although my business continues to make a satisfactory return, the long-term prospects are uncertain. For this reason, I have decided to seek full-time employment with a well established large company, strong enough to hold its own in this highly competitive field.

(Assuming, of course, that this is the case, as it so often will be.)

For guidance on how the rest of the letter might read, attention should be paid to the chapter entitled, 'The Introductory Letter'.

Question: *What does the applicant put on his CV if he is currently out of work, following release from prison?*

Answer: I subscribe to the belief that he who is half clever enough to tell a lie will be clever enough to know better than to try it. Although it is known for applicants in this situation to make false statements, e.g. long-term unemployed, working for a friend, working overseas etc., the truth could emerge at an interview, or through a prospective employer making a thorough check on an individual's background.

     Any applicant feeling inclined to attempt concealing a period of imprisonment should remember that it is a statutory offence to obtain employment by deception. Surely he would be better to be open about it and contend that his debt to society has been paid, and he intends to apply himself with great dedication, in order to regain the respect of his fellow beings?

Question: *Should those with disabilities disclose the fact on their CV?*

Answer: If an applicant is a registered disabled person, this should be entered in the personal details section.

Question: *I have been working continuously for the*

*past fifteen years, but for most of the last
seven I have been doing two jobs at once.
How do I accommodate these in my CV?*

Answer: It is probable that, in this situation, the
applicant will have been working as a full-
time employee for one organisation and, in
his spare time, as a part-time employee for
one, or several other employers. Assuming
the part-time experience to be relevant to
the kind of work being sought, it should be
dealt with immediately below the full-time
career history, which will be set out in the
usual way. After this, will appear:

Part-time Work Experience
– which will also run in reverse date order.

    Unless the part-time work in question is
of special importance, you should think
hard before including it. The prospective
employer might decide that if you continued
with part-time work after joining him,
your attention would be divided between
the two jobs. This would certainly deter
him, even if his fears were unjustified.

Question: *I am eighteen years old and have a full-time,
unskilled job working in a slaughterhouse.
Despite having obtained quite good GCSE
grades, I see no chance of improving my
career prospects.*

    *I have been advised to go back into full-
time education and get some more
qualifications, then my CV would look much
more appealing. What do you think?*

Answer: Go back into education and study for two
good 'A' Level grades in solid subjects.
These will command widespread respect

from prospective employers reading your CV. Be wary of the marketing skills of institutions selling and running a range of alternative courses, some of which are looked upon with suspicion by employers.

Question: *I am forty and, although I have extensive experience in my work, I have little in the way of formal qualifications. I find this very discouraging when trying to write my CV. What should I do?*

Answer: Take heart. One of the best CVs I have ever written was for an engineer, whose only qualifications were his indentures. Some twenty years previously he had served a five year apprenticeship with an old established company, running its own, carefully devised in-house apprentice training scheme. This man, whose achievements were awesome, represented an outstanding example of qualification by experience.

Provided your CV lands on the right desk, all the reader will want to know is what you have done in your work. This will enable him to decide what you can do for him.

If your CV lands on the wrong desk, it will be read by a 'personnel professional', who might have little understanding of what he is reading. In the absence of a decorative array of certificates and diplomas, he will toss it aside with contempt.

You could also come to grief at the hands of a recruitment consultant who, until a fortnight earlier, might have been selling baked beans.

Obviously, your chances will be much better where someone with experience in your trade is involved in the recruitment process. This is more likely where a company is doing its own recruiting.

Question: *A colleague says that when a friend of his was writing his CV, he prefaced the career history with a brief statement, i.e.:*
'A self-motivated and successful Sales Professional, able to apply his superbly developed interpersonal skills to attain maximum levels of profitable business growth, in the highly charged and challenging environment of a dynamic industrial/commercial, import/export organisation'.
What would you say to that?

Answer: I would say that this man is an unprincipled line shooter, who should go into politics at national level where he will have a bright future.

The question highlights the growing tendency by people and organisations in all walks of life, to speak and write in pretentious jargon instead of making clear, simple statements.

This is the gloss culture, which has spread out from its origins in the world of advertising, to infiltrate the whole of the public services sector and large areas of industry and commerce, with devastating consequences. If you allow the gloss culture to creep into your CV, you are in grave danger of being identified with its two main objectives, i.e. the concealment of poor standards and the glorification of mediocrity.

Question: *I have prepared what I believe to be a*

perfectly good CV, but the job I am applying for requires me to complete an application form. Should I attach a copy of my CV to the application form and write on it – See enclosed CV?

Answer: No. Whilst a properly prepared CV can be expected to provide two-thirds to three-quarters of the information required on most application forms, there will still be questions, often very important ones, which must be answered. I suggest the following way of dealing with this common problem: all questions relating to personal details, education, qualifications and training should be answered in the usual way, although it will often mean writing down again details which are already in the CV. Then read through the form carefully and answer any questions which are not catered for by the CV.

Where the career history or employment experience is concerned, the form may have only a relatively small area in which to insert the briefest of details, in which case, that is what must be done. However, when the form concludes with one, two or even more blank pages for details of previous employment, it is common practice to write – See enclosed CV – and attach a copy.

Consider also the problem of the large organisation which might distribute hundreds of returned application forms between several senior executives, with instructions to compile a list for first interview. Suppose that, say, question 10 is the important one. Visualise the difficulty if applicants have answered it by advising scrutiny of an attached CV. For this reason, some applicants frequently complete the application form in its entirety, particularly when the post on offer happens to be in the state sector.

It comes down in the end to an accurate assessment of each individual situation, e.g. size of company, type of business, kind of work being applied for.

Question: *I am in senior management and I am applying for a similar position, with better long-term prospects. I have been told that I should place a copy of my CV in a presentation folder, then send it in a matching sized envelope. But others say that this is going too far and if I do it the CV will be discarded with contempt because they will think I am a big-head. What should I do?*

Answer: For applicants in senior management, or in sales and marketing, presentation is of considerable importance. As in all things, views differ about what constitutes a pleasing presentation. Among the many job applicants I meet, it has become the norm for those who need to present themselves in this way to use an A4 'see through' perspex folder with a slim plastic spine clip. To complete the process, the CV should have a face (or front) page. In the centre of the face page should be typed:

CURRICULUM VITAE
OF
FORENAME(S) SURNAME

When the CV has been inserted securely in the folder, the introductory letter (see

Chapter 8) should be clipped to the outside, and the whole package placed in an A4 envelope.

Question: *After my employer closed down, I was unemployed for over a year. I have now undergone retraining as an audio typist. How do I explain this interlude on my CV?*

Answer: Assuming the course took up a reasonable slice of the period of unemployment, the entry on your CV might read thus:

Nov. (year)   Took advantage of this period of
– Oct. (year)   unemployment to retrain, with a view to acquiring greater versatility.

(Details of this course will already have been inserted under education, qualifications and training.)

Question: *But I am confessing to a long period of unemployment. Surely that will ruin my prospects?*

Answer: You have shown that you are sufficiently self-motivated to have improved your range of skills, in order to get off the dole. If you conceal this period of unemployment by telling lies, you are in fact confessing in writing to an offence you have not committed, i.e. working whilst drawing unemployment benefit.

Question: *How long should a CV be?*

Answer: This brings us back into the territory of the baked bean selling recruitment consultant, the personnel professional and everyone else involved in human resource management (a typical example of gloss culturespeak). These, and other 'experts', will invariably tell you that on no account must your CV exceed two A4 pages. Their advice will be damaging in many cases.

The majority of CVs that I have prepared are on three A4 pages of paper. Most of the remainder are on two or four pages, with a very small number exceeding four pages. In common with seasoned campaigners who have lived and worked in places across the world, I do not like to see a CV exceed three pages. Unfortunately, this cannot be taken as a hard and fast rule.

Consider the typical example of an applicant who is already in management, and is applying for a better paid job with even more responsibility than at present. He needs to give a comprehensive account of his experience and could well find that keeping down to three pages will do more harm than going onto a fourth.

Faced with a CV on, say, three and a half A4 pages, I have debated the question, 'Do we cut it down, or do we leave it?', with many job applicants, and the answer is not always the same. But there has to be a convincing reason for allowing the CV to encroach onto a fourth page. Applicants in this situation should do their utmost to keep down to three pages, but not by attempting to cram too much information onto each sheet. This leaves the reader hunting around in search of important material and he will lose patience. Do not try to 'cheat', by using small type and narrow margins. This will only make a quick initial scan difficult or, where the reader is 'visually challenged', downright impossible.

Consider also the young student or graduate, whose CV should not really exceed two A4 pages. A large amount of part-time work for numerous employers, coupled with an extensive academic record and the names and addresses of two referees, makes a two page presentation an unrealistic goal. Here again you have to do your best, but be careful not to undersell yourself.

Question: *Should I send a photograph with my CV?*

Answer: Usually an applicant will only enclose a photograph when requested to do so, e.g. when applying for a job as an air hostess, or any other position where appearance is all important.

Question: *But I am an attractive twenty-two year old female, applying for a job as a dental nurse. Although the advertisement does not ask for a photograph, surely it could make all the difference, could it not?*

Answer: Indeed it could, especially if the dentist's wife is helping him to vet the applications. In that case, being of middle age and blessed with great ugliness could be virtues of a high order.

8
THE INTRODUCTORY LETTER

When replying to an advertisement for a job vacancy, the CV must always be accompanied by an introductory letter.

The quality of the letter is at least as important as the quality of the CV, in some cases more so. Applicants who are equipped with a good CV might fail repeatedly to secure an invitation to attend an interview because of a bad letter.

Remember that the letter is the opening shot. It creates the first impression which is the one by which most people judge. An impressive letter can overcome the odd weakness in a CV. Conversely, a poor letter might cause a perfectly good CV to be thrown in the waste-bin.

The letter must be short, crisp and clear, opening with the name and date of issue of the publication in which the advertisement appeared. If a reference number is given, it should be displayed in the top left-hand corner of the letter and likewise, on the envelope.

In the second paragraph, the applicant should say briefly why he believes that he is a suitable candidate for the job.

The third paragraph should contain a good reason why that job is particularly desirable.

The concluding part of the letter should supply routine information, e.g. current rate of pay if the advertisement requests this; period of notice required by present employer, and the length of notice needed to attend an interview.

The letter should reflect the kind of person from whom the recruiter is hoping to hear. This requirement is clearly illustrated in the three specimen letters below:

From a plumber

> 5 Avenue Road,
> Anytown,
> Midshire,
> XX1 1YY

Mr P A Scott-Brown,   Date
Adapt Mechanical Services Ltd,
118–120 Hunts Road,
Anytown,
Midshire,
XX1 1YY

Dear Sir,

I have seen your advertisement, in the Construction Gazette of July 8th, for plumbers to work on a Dutch chemical factory contract.

My experience includes work of a similar kind, e.g. the Cann Chemical Factory in Nigeria, for Hull & Blackwell Ltd.

Having just completed a hospital building contract in Saudi Arabia as a Foreman Plumber with Bates, Barlow (Construction) Ltd, I am now looking for the kind of work offered by your advertisement.

A copy of my CV is enclosed and, if you decide to see me for an interview, I could attend at short notice.

> Yours faithfully,
>
> Martin Smith

Let us change now from the purely practical style of the tradesman to what might be expected of the high-powered, young executive burning with ambition.

Your Ref: XX 111

5 The Close,
Anytown,
Midshire,
XX1 1YY

Mr P R Whiteside,   Date
Personnel Manager,
Wayside Box & Packaging Co Ltd,
6–10 Wayside,
Anytown,
Midshire,
XX1 1YY

Dear Sir,

Your advertisement in the Daily Post of May 12th for a
Regional Sales Manager to increase the rate of business
growth in the Southern Counties is of great interest to me.

You will see from the enclosed CV that I have had
extensive experience in negotiating at all levels, including
much successful sharp end contact.

Whilst relations with my employers remain very good,
the job does not hold the same prospect of advancement
that would exist in a larger organisation.

My employers would require one month's notice of
leaving. I would appreciate the opportuty of an interview, and it would help if I could have three working days'
notice of the date.

Yours faithfully,

James Smith

Changing the style yet again, we see what someone applying for a clerical job might write.

29 Brook Avenue
Anytown,
Midshire,
XX1 1YY

Reville, Walker & Bates   Date
Chartered Architects,
173 Avondale Road,
Anytown,
Midshire,
XX1 1YY

Dear Sirs,
   I would like to be considered for the position of Secretary/Typist, advertised in the Daily Gazette of April 8th.
   A copy of my CV is enclosed, and you will see that in addition to my RSA Word Processing Certificate, I do have the required GCSE grades in English and Mathematics. I also have three years' experience as a secretary/typist.
   With having moved into the area only recently, I am looking for permanent employment in secretarial work, where the duties and responsibilities would be similar to those in my last job (salary £xx,xxx).
   The opportunity of an interview would be much appreciated, and I could attend at short notice.

Yours faithfully,
Julie Brown

   Although these three specimen letters display clearly the necessary differences in style, they should only be viewed as a loose guide since, in order to draft an introductory job application letter accurately, you need the advertisement before you.

9
THE SPECULATIVE APPROACH

Many job seekers pass the time between applying for advertised vacancies by 'blitzing' companies in a particular field of activity. An advantage of using this ploy is that once drafted, the same letter can be used repeatedly. The disadvantage is that the process amounts to a series of long shots in the dark, and some employers have become ill-disposed to such treatment.

However, if this course of action is to be taken, it must be done properly. The first step is to decide which organisations to approach. Compile an initial list of (say) ten companies. Discover the names and job titles of the company officials to whom the letter is to be addressed.

I emphasise the importance of identifying the individual personnel manager, recruiting officer, head of department, etc. If this is not done, or done wrong, the application may not find its way to the right person. Even if it does, he will not give it as much weight as he would when seeing his name on the envelope, as well as on the letter.

A brief telephone call to each of the companies selected is usually all that is necessary, since the switchboard operator is likely to be able to supply the name and job title of the official concerned. Items for special attention are his initials, and the correct spelling of his name.

Having set the stage, next comes the composition of the letter which need be little more than a courteous introduction, with a view to being placed on file.

6 The Avenue
Anytown,
Midshire,
XX1 1YY

Mr J A Smith,   Date
Personnel Manager,
Wayside Chemical Products Ltd,
18–22 Wayside,
Anytown,
Midshire,
XX1 1YY

Dear Sir,

   Although you may not have any vacancies advertised at the moment, I am writing to ask if you might be able to offer me a position as a chemical research analyst.

   The enclosed CV will show that, in addition to possessing the necessary qualifications, I have gained a broad range of experience, which I am sure could be used to advantage in working for your company.

   My employers require one month's notice of leaving. I would appreciate the opportunity of an interview if a vacancy occurs, and five working days' notice would be helpful.

Yours faithfully

Peter Bailey

   When the job application, or speculative approach, letter has been composed, one question still remains: should it be typed or handwritten?

   When replying to an advertised vacancy, this question will sometimes already have been answered, e.g. where applicants are required to apply in their own handwriting. The usual response, in this case, is to enclose a hand-written letter with a copy of the CV, although some applicants go the whole hog, and hand copy their CV as well. The merits of such eagerness to please are at best debatable, except where the advertisement specifies a handwritten CV.

Applicants who have reached senior management level will often dismiss any suggestion of handwritten correspondence, preferring to offer a business-like presentation.

Sometimes a male applicant will ask his partner to write the letter, or complete the job application form as the partner's handwriting is neater than the applicant's. No doubt this practice has caused the odd furrowed brow in the world of graphology!

HOW NOT TO WRITE A JOB APPLICATION LETTER

> 6 Firtree Grove,
> Anytown,
> Midshire,
> XX1 1YY

The Manager,   Date
Anytown Saw-Mills Ltd,
Anytown Industrial Estate,
Anytown,
Midshire,
XX1 1YY

Dear Sir,

I believe you are looking for an office manager, and I think I could be the man for the job.

The enclosed CV will show you what I am capable of. From it, you will see that I have had wide experience in managing offices in many different industries, and I believe this is the only way to learn.

Living as I do very close to your premises, I would appear to be ideally located, and I should be pleased to attend an interview if you should very kindly invite me to one.

Yours faithfully,

Jim Brown

The opening of this letter is too casual. If the applicant has heard that there is a job vacancy with the company, he should locate the advertisement and apply in the normal way. If, on the other hand, he has heard secretly from a friend that there might be a position open but no advertisement has yet been placed, he should try a speculative approach.

The applicant continues in a high-handed manner, telling the reader to see 'what I am capable of' and then goes on to say, 'I believe this is the only way to learn'. Who does he think he is? This statement clearly implies that the reader would be wrong to disagree.

In emphasising that his home is near to their place of business, the applicant obviously believes this will strengthen his case. The opposite could be just as easily implied. He has made it clear that his main reason for applying is that it would be a convenient place for him to go to work.

Finally, after sailing through nearly the whole of the letter in this haughty manner, the applicant suddenly turns to the other extreme. He starts to crawl, by saying with regard to an interview, 'if you should very kindly invite me to one'. The reader will be left with an easy decision, and this sickening letter will rightly end up in the waste-bin.

AND FINALLY

Although this book is bound to help some more than others, it is hard to see how anyone in the job market who has read it completely can have failed to learn something of value.

While many job applicants ruin their prospects by trying too hard and appearing boastful, a similar number wreck their chances by selling themselves short. This is the modesty factor. It prevents the applicant from giving a good account of himself, but may go deeper, and cause him even to be unaware of the many useful qualities he possesses.

Just one of the aims in writing this book has been to try and show the reader how to make the good first impression, which is so vitally important. Even if the job being sought does not exactly match an applicant's career background, a good presentation might cause the recruiter to say, 'He isn't exactly what we have in mind, but he certainly seems like a chap worth meeting. I think we'll have him in for a chat'.

In the end, it comes down to being as sure as you can be, that your CV is a concise, factual and attractive document.

INDEX

OUR PUBLISHING POLICY

HOW WE CHOOSE

Our policy is to consider every deserving manuscript and we can give special editorial help where an author is an authority on his subject but an inexperienced writer. We are rigorously selective in the choice of books we publish. We set the highest standards of editorial quality and accuracy. This means that a *Paperfront* is easy to understand and delightful to read. Where illustrations are necessary to convey points of detail, these are drawn up by a subject specialist artist from our panel.

HOW WE KEEP PRICES LOW

We aim for the big seller. This enables us to order enormous print runs and achieve the lowest price for you. Unfortunately, this means that you will not find in the *Paperfront* list any titles on obscure subjects of minority interest only. These could not be printed in large enough quantities to be sold for the low price at which we offer this series.

We sell almost all our *Paperfronts* at the same unit price. This saves a lot of fiddling about in our clerical departments and helps us to give you world-beating value. Under this system, the longer titles are offered at a price which we believe to be unmatched by any publisher in the world.

OUR DISTRIBUTION SYSTEM

Because of the competitive price, and the rapid turnover, *Paperfronts* are possibly the most profitable line a bookseller can handle. They are stocked by the best bookshops all over the world. It may be that your bookseller has run out of stock of a particular title. If so, he can order more from us at any time – we have a fine reputation for "same day" despatch, and we supply any order, however small (even a single copy), to any bookseller who has an account with us. We prefer you to buy from your bookseller, as this reminds him of the strong underlying public demand for *Paperfronts*. Members of the public who live in remote places, or who are housebound, or whose local bookseller is unco-operative, can order direct from us by post.

FREE

If you would like an up-to-date list of all *Paperfront* titles currently available, please send a stamped self-addressed envelope to ELLIOT RIGHT WAY BOOKS, BRIGHTON RD., LOWER KINGSWOOD, TADWORTH, SURREY, U.K.